Secrets to Surviving Your Children's Love Relationships

Also by Dr. Terri Orbuch

5 Simple Steps to Take Your Marriage from Good to Great
Finding Love Again: 6 Simple Steps to a New and Happy Relationship
Thrice Told Tales: Married Couples Tell Their Stories

Secrets to Surviving Your Children's Love Relationships

A Guide for Parents

Terri Orbuch, PhD
The Love Doctor®

PARENT **READY**

PARENT **READY**

Parent Ready
8 East Windsor Avenue
Alexandria, Virginia 22301
https://parentready.com

First Parent Ready trade paperback edition March 2022

Parent Ready and design are trademarks of Parent Ready Inc.

Bulk purchase special discounts are available. Please make inquiries via
https://relationshipsecrets.guide.

Interior design by Kathleen Dyson

Library of Congress Cataloging-in-Publication Data has been applied for.

ISBN: 978-1-7369182-9-6 (paperback)
ISBN: 978-1-7369182-8-9 (ebook)

Advance Praise for *Secrets to Surviving Your Children's Love Relationships*

"Dr. Terri Orbuch is the real deal. She brings the best of scientific knowledge to the challenge of preparing your children for present and future relationships. I can't think of a parent who couldn't use her practical quizzes and advice."**—PEPPER SCHWARTZ, PhD, Professor of Sociology, University of Washington**

"Guess what? Parenting doesn't end when our kids turn 18. Enter Terri Orbuch. In this truly unique resource, she offers clear, supportive, *crucial* advice on how to guide our young adults in one of the single most important aspects of their future well-being: establishing healthy, happy, fulfilling relationships."**—PEGGY ORENSTEIN, *New York Times* best-selling author of *Girls & Sex* and *Boys & Sex***

"Dr. Terri Orbuch delivers another masterclass on how to approach our intimate lives with care, compassion, and scientific evidence. With her remarkable knack for weaving decades of research into approachable and realistic take-aways that we can implement in our relationships, Orbuch focuses her lens on the enduring power of parent-child bonds. In this delightful book, she provides a guide for parents of all backgrounds to support their adult children along their journey to love."**—DR. JUSTIN GARCIA, Executive Director of the Kinsey Institute at Indiana University & Scientific Advisor to Match**

"Help your kids grow up to find and keep a lifetime of love! This easy-to-use book by the foremost scientist on long-term love shows you exactly how. And bonus! Your own relationship will be happier, too."**—DUANA C. WELCH, PhD, author of *Love Factually: 10 Proven Steps from I Wish to I Do***

"*Secrets to Surviving Your Children's Love Relationships* gives parents science-based information to help their children enjoy healthy relationships. Packed with practical tools, tips, conversation starters, and activities, this must-have book will help parents and children better navigate relationships now and in the future."**—GARY W. LEWANDOWSKI JR. PhD, author of *Stronger Than You Think***

"An essential read for parents. Orbuch writes in an accessible, down-to-earth style that seamlessly weaves science, personal anecdotes, and practical tips. The end result is an indispensable guide to helping your children not only survive but thrive in their relationships."**—JUSTIN J. LEHMILLER, Ph.D., Kinsey Institute Research Fellow and author of *Tell Me What You Want***

*To Abigail and Joshua—Wishing you relationships
that are filled with love and happiness.
I am grateful to be your mother!*

Contents

Acknowledgments

There are many people whose assistance and support have made this book possible. First, I would like to thank all of the participants in the Early Years of Marriage (EYM) study and my online parent survey on relationship conversations. I also am thankful for all of the students and colleagues who work passionately on the EYM project. I am indebted to my colleague and friend Dr. Joseph Veroff, whose initial vision drove the EYM study and who invited me to be a part of this innovative project. I also greatly appreciate my colleagues, friends, and students at Oakland University, who have encouraged, supported, and affirmed me and my work. I am proud to be a part of the Oakland University community as a Distinguished Professor.

I want to thank Dan Solomon, founder and CEO of Wise Action, who was dedicated and enthusiastic about this book project from the beginning and assisted me in many ways throughout the process. I am also thankful for Anja Schmidt's insights, careful editing, and writing skills; my copyeditor for her thorough work; Kathleen Dyson for her creative design of the book; Marlena Brown, who facilitates publicity for the book; and Kiki Sayre and Jae Beckmeyer, who helped with fact-checking, research reviews, and other important contributions to the book. I also want to acknowledge the support and collaboration of my colleagues from the International Association for Relationship Research (IARR).

Most important to mention are my personal relationships that inspire and motivate me, and mean the world to me. My parents,

Joyce and Marty—you have been amazing role models of generosity, communication, and an example of a healthy love relationship. Thank you for your love and support. To my children, Abigail and Joshua—I appreciate your caring and lovingness. You bring me such joy and I am so proud of the adults you have become. To my sister Debra, brother David, and good friends, I value our friendship and I am very fortunate to have each and every one of you in my life. And to Stuart—my husband and partner in parenting—I am grateful and blessed to walk this journey of life with you. You have always been by my side, cheering loudly, and you have helped my dreams and passions become a reality.

Introduction

Over two decades ago, when my first child was born and the nurse placed her small, swaddled body in my arms, I looked in wonder at this new person and tried to imagine who she would become. With all the fervor of a protective new mother, I whispered to her that I would do whatever I could to make her life a happy one. A few years later, at the birth of my son, I made the same vow to him. While my conviction was just as strong with my second child, the short time I'd spent as a parent gave me a glimpse into the real challenges to fulfilling my promise.

My wish for my children wasn't original. Every parent hopes to provide the best possible lives for their children. We want them to be healthy and happy, make good decisions in life, feel positive and confident in the people they become, and have close and fulfilling love relationships. And, particularly in their love relationships, we want to give our children a strong measure of self-efficacy—a sense that they are capable of producing the outcomes they want.

We also expect that we'll have a lifelong, enjoyable relationship with our children as they grow older. We want them to feel comfortable to come and talk to us about their challenges and struggles, visit with us over the holidays, listen to our advice and warnings, and of course—we dream about getting along with (and liking) their love partners.

Now my children are both young adults. I am finished with toilet training, the terrible twos, and nightmares about monsters in the closets. These days, what I think about is their place in the world with others. Are their current obstacles and stressors more challenging and crucial than when they were young? Are the decisions they make now the ones that will really define them as people? How can I guide them to choose friends and love partners who are the best for them personally and who will treat them with respect and kindness? What do I want to model and discuss for their futures, particularly in terms of their love relationships? And most importantly, how can I navigate a happy, healthy relationship with them into the future? While I haven't given up on my promise, I certainly have way more to think about now to help ensure their happiness. In fact, when my kids were young, I would hear other parents say, "Little kids, little problems. Big kids, big problems," more times than I can count. But until my children became young adults, I just could not fully grasp what that meant.

It is no accident that you've opened this book. You probably have a young adult child and are asking the same questions that I am. Your child may be dating and experiencing the challenges of heartbreak or not finding that someone special. They* may be going through adolescence and discovering romantic love for the first time, or they're older and partnered with someone who you're convinced isn't right for them.

Whether you're reacting to a present relationship challenge or you're interested in laying the groundwork for your children's love relationships and a lifelong bond with them, *this book is for YOU!* This book is a *must read* if you want your children to grow up and have healthy, happy relationships of their own. This is a vital point in your journey as a parent. The stakes are high and most importantly, *you have the POWER to change* your children's love relationships, and at the same time, pave the road to a better lifelong relationship with your children. Sure, that journey will be strewn with roadblocks

---

* I use the pronoun they in its singular form throughout the book because it is the most practical and inclusive approach.

along the way (which we will discuss) but seize the moment *now* to make that journey and those good relationships possible.

In this book, I'll distill science-based information and present it in the form of highly practical tips, scripts, quizzes, and easy-to-understand approaches for guiding your children in choosing the kinds of healthy, happy relationships that can make their lives more fulfilling. These positive, simple strategies will help you to talk to your children about relationships, regardless of their age and gender, as well as provide tips to examine your own relationships and interactions with other people so that you can model and provide positive examples for your children. I recognize that these kinds of discussions may not be easy for you, and you may even be confronted with some resistance from your children. This is common; *do not worry.* In this book, you will learn how to build up the trust in the relationship first (Chapter 1), ask the right questions (Chapter 2), affirm your child's strengths (Chapter 3), and change the way you speak (Chapter 4) so that the conversations are less challenging, and your children feel comfortable sharing with you. In addition, the themes in each of the chapters in this book tackle the most important relationship issues and can help you confidently and competently approach them with your children.

GOOD RELATIONSHIPS FOR YOUR CHILDREN START WITH YOU

You already know intuitively that healthy love relationships make a tremendous difference in the quality of our lives. When we are in happy, loving relationships, we're better able to handle stress, more likely to be physically active, less likely to be depressed and suffer from illnesses, and, in general, live longer, healthier lives. Scientific studies support the idea that there is nothing more important than healthy relationships. They determine almost everything in our lives and have profound effects on our physical and mental health. I'll discuss more about these studies and the importance of healthy relationships on overall health in future chapters.

I know one of the best shots I can give my kids to help ensure their happiness is to teach them the importance of healthy relationships, what they look like, and how to have them. More specifically, I tell my young adult children that at first blush, a relationship can be passionate and exciting, but "real" deep love comes years later, after weathering trials and tribulations, many disagreements, and life's ups and downs together. I also want them to understand that remaining optimistic and positive is essential, because those personality qualities will attract many potential relationship partners. People attract what they give out into the world. And, of course, I also want them to understand that being happy and confident with themselves is the key ingredient to relationship happiness and stability.

As parents, we have a responsibility, both through conversation and example, to provide our children with the relationship skills, information, and tools to make healthy decisions on their own. Although this book is geared to parents who have young adult children aged 16–28, it is never too late (or too early) to start these behavior changes and discussions. Giving our children information and teaching them skills for having healthy love relationships are the most significant tools we can share with them to help them have happy, healthy lives. That's why I wanted to write this book.

I understand the importance of these tools, not only as a mother who's made a promise to my own kids, but as a professional therapist and coach, and most significantly, as the director of the longest running scientific study on love relationships spanning 373 couples over 30 years (more on the Early Years of Marriage (EYM) study in a bit). No one has the insight and access I have from this study and no other book out there draws on actual scientific research to, in turn, prove that my methods are true and will work.

The insights I've gleaned from my research and experience are incredibly valuable—and incredibly important—for everyone. Through all my research and counseling, learning from my own experience as a mother, and from watching my own parents, I can tell you with authority: **good relationships for your children *start with you*.** When I do workshops, parents say things to me like, "My kids are still single, and I want to help them find a good partner and be confident. How can I model with my own partner to help them?" My answer is always the same: You can't guarantee good relationships for your children (just like good parenting doesn't assure healthy functioning behaviors for your children), but you *do* set the tone for how to find happiness from and in their relationships.

Modeling behavior and having conversations with your children about healthy relationships will give them the tools to make better decisions about relationships for themselves, now and later in life. The relationship behaviors you model in your own relationships influence how your kids view relationships, how they interact with others, and how they view conflict. In my therapy practice, I see adults who come in and realize how the experiences that went on in their childhood—surrounding money, conflict, household chores, interactions between parents—really affects them.

Through modeling and conversations, you can also improve the quality of the bond that you have with your children, now and into the future. When you make relationships a topic of conversation with your children, they become more comfortable coming to you with personal questions, issues, and/or challenges. These conversations, in turn, build trust between you and your children, and help alleviate the fears we all face as parents when our children venture into the world to make their own decisions and choices. In other words, the conversations you have now will determine the relationship you have with your children into the future!

It's important to understand that helping your children develop healthy relationships of their own is only partly affected by what you *say* to them. The most important thing is how you show—or model—healthy behaviors in your *own* relationships. You are their model, their standard, and their example for how to act, think, and talk in interacting with others, especially in their love relationships. They listen to what you say to them, but they are more influenced by what they watch and observe in your interactions within your own close relationships—and even your acquaintances. For example, studies show that your casual friends and acquaintances are the glue that holds your day-to-day life together. These relationships also deserve your attention and consideration. Show small acts of kindness to these acquaintances. Make an effort to connect with these people and get to know them a little more as people. Instead of rushing by your neighbor, delivery person, or receptionist at the doctor's office, slow down and talk to them—in front of your children. Do you know the person's first name? Do you make eye contact and greet people? Do you open the door for someone? These acts of kindness will influence how your kids treat their love partners as well.

We know that fights in any relationship are inevitable. But learning how to fight fair is critical to building a healthy relationship. Findings from the EYM study show that it's not how *much* you fight, but *how* you fight that's important to whether you'll stay together over the long haul. My research supports the idea that couples who know how to fight are more likely to stay together. If you resolve conflict using destructive behaviors—yelling, screaming, interrupting, bringing up the past—it will lead to trouble in your relationship. If you deal with the conflict using constructive behaviors—listening, validating each other's emotions, taking a break to remain calm—you're much more likely to stay together and be happy.

How you fight in front of your children will change the way your kids think about and behave in relationships. I know it sounds crazy, but you *need* to fight in front of your kid. It's a myth that you shouldn't, and I want to dispel that misconception. When couples fight well and resolve the disagreement in front of their kids, the kids learn that fighting is part of a healthy relationship, and they won't run at the first sign of conflict in their own relationships. In Chapter 4, I'll give you the tools for how to fight fair, how to communicate with each other, and how to end disagreements without stress—and in a loving way—so that you can model them correctly. Your kids will learn that people who love and care about each other sometimes fight and they will know how to do it in a healthy way in their own relationships.

What about how your kids view money? What money symbolizes is developed in childhood. For example, if your parent wasn't around much, they might have bought you gifts instead, so money for you represents love. Or if you grew up without much money, it represents stability and security and you remember that when your family had it, your parents were relaxed and didn't fight much. Or if your parents talked about gaining money in a positive way, it might be a sign of how well you're doing, so it becomes part of your ego. You take that meaning into your love relationships without even realizing it. It's also the #1 source of conflict in relationships. I know from my EYM study that 75% of couples say money produces tension in their relationship. It's not the money you're arguing about—it's the meaning it represents. In Chapter 6 I'll give you the tools to understand what you're teaching your children about money and how it can affect their love relationships, and the relationship you have with them long-term.

MY STORY

About 17 years ago, I was listening to Dr. Phil, and he was giving out some relationship advice to a couple. He said, "You have to make sure that you don't fight in front of your children, and you don't fight as a couple." It made me think about my experience as a therapist, professor, and scientist. I had just analyzed some of my own research that supported the theory that the happy couples in my study and the couples who had stayed together were the ones who actually learned how to fight well. In fact, there were 12 couples in Years 1 and 3 in my study who said that they never fought, never had any conflict, never disagreed with their partner—and none of those couples were still together by Year 4. As I ran through this data analysis in my head, I thought to myself, "Oh, he is so incorrect. He is giving incorrect information to these people and on-air for thousands of other couples just like them to hear."

I knew I had to do something. I made it my mission to take these scientific findings and translate them into understandable, accessible, and actionable knowledge that people can easily incorporate into their own lives in *all* of their relationships. Over the past 17 years, and in previous books, I've perfected the art of taking that information and boiling it down to make people quickly realize, "A-ha! I can do this!" I became The Love Doctor®. I built a brand to get this science-based information out in an easily digestible way. I started to do radio and television appearances. I wrote articles and blog posts. I took any and every opportunity to be The Love Doctor® to provide people the best, most accurate information about the keys to successful relationships.

In my career, I wear several hats, but the common denominator for each of my professional pursuits is observing interpersonal relationships. I am a Distinguished Professor of Sociology at Oakland University, a research scientist at the University of Michigan Institute for Social Research, and the lead researcher in a long-term study of marriage and divorce funded by the National Institutes of Health (NIH). I am in private practice as a marriage and family counselor and a dating and relationship coach to singles and couples around the world. As The Love Doctor®, I am a relationship expert and advisor to TV, radio, print, and online audiences. And I am a wife of 29 years and a mother of two.

After listening to the same questions and concerns again and again from my research participants, therapy and coaching clients, radio and TV audiences, workshop participants, and students, I noticed a common theme: Parents really want the knowledge to be able to help their kids have good relationships. What can they do? What can they say? And most concerning, I have discovered that too few parents have *any* conversations about relationships with their children.

THE SCIENCE BEHIND MY ADVICE

Let me back up a bit. What is this study that makes me the most trusted expert in the field? The Early Years of Marriage (EYM) study began in 1986 as a four-year study, funded by NIH, to identify what keeps marriages together and happy, and what breaks marriages apart. Recognizing the wealth of information gleaned in the first four years, the EYM has continued to receive NIH funding through the years, expanding far beyond the "early years" of marriage. In fact, the study has been going on for 30 years and continues today—it is the longest running study of its kind in the United States. I have followed 373 couples—just over half of whom are still married to their original spouse (46% are divorced)—and have gleaned incredible insights about how external stressors (such as money, employment, and in-laws), and internal relationship factors (such as sexuality, conflict, and communication) affect marital happiness and longevity.

AT A GLANCE: Background on the National Institutes of Health EYM Study

The participants in the Early Years of Marriage (EYM) project are married couples, who applied for marriage licenses in a particular Midwest county over a three-month period, and who agreed to take part in the study. I have followed 373 couples for over 30 years—just under half of whom (46%) are no longer married to their original spouse.[1]

The EYM study was designed to:

- Study married couples who represent typical North American couples from all walks of life.

- Observe the same 373 couples over time (now 746 individuals, about half of whom are still married to the same spouse and about half of whom are no longer married to the same spouse).

- Collect information from both members of the couple separately, as well as together.

- Examine what keeps couples together and happy, and what breaks them apart.

For example, when it came to external stressors, working spouses who are happy in their jobs are more likely to be happy in their marriages, which emphasizes the positive spillover from work to relationship. Surprisingly, income and class weren't predictors of happiness, but when couples have high financial stress (you can be a millionaire and still be stressed), couples are less likely to stay together.

For internal stressors, couples who continue to see marriage in an overly romantic way are less happy and less likely to know how to deal with stressful situations because they are overly idealistic (from their childhood, their parents, the media, etc.). Boredom also eats away at happiness; all relationships have what I call "relationship ruts"—routine, habits—but if a rut lasts for too long, partners become unhappy. Also, study after study says to add newness to your relationship, which puts the excitement of the beginning back into the relationship. Go to a new vacation spot or change date night. My husband and I have taken a four-week cooking class together, enjoyed a salsa dance class, and joined a gym together—all new activities that brought the excitement and passion back into our marriage.

And if these stressors are important to healthy relationships, then they are certainly critical to help inform your kids about their own love relationships. Oftentimes, parents aren't on solid footing for giving relationship advice or information because they never had these kinds of conversations or saw these behaviors with their own parents. Alternatively, many parents may have learned myths or information that is not supported by science (discussed further in Chapter 1). I asked parents from across the country about their experiences, by posting an online survey on my website. The goal was to augment the contents of this book. One of the questions asked whether the parents of the respondent ever "discussed relationships or what it means to be in a good relationship" when the respondent was growing up. It is telling that 53 of the 60 respondents answered "No." Many of the comments accompanying their answers were along the lines of: "Other than telling us to be respectful, in general, and to never have sex until we're married, they never really explained much about relationships." The majority of parents who responded to my online survey received *no advice* about relationships when they were young. Now they're grappling with how they can have an effect on their own children's love relationships.

AT A GLANCE: Online Parent Survey on Relationship Conversations

In planning the contents of this book, I asked parents, through an online survey posted on my website, to share their own experiences with learning about relationships and discussing relationships with their children. The survey consisted of 10 brief questions and was voluntary and completely anonymous. I recruited or asked for volunteers to participate in the online survey on my "Love Doctor" social media channels (e.g., Twitter, Facebook, newsletter). The solicitation mentioned that as a researcher, I needed parents, 18 years or older, to participate in an online research study. Over its three-month posting, it elicited 60 responses. Demographically, the respondents represented:

- Age span: 23–84 years old

- Gender: 51 women; 9 men

- Marital status: 45 married; 9 divorced; 3 separated; 3 never married

- Number of children: 13 one child; 26 two; 17 three; 4 four

- Ages of children: 4 months–60 years old; mean age: 16

In addition, several of the online survey respondents commented that, while their parents didn't discuss relationships with them, their parents modeled relationship lessons through both positive and negative examples. "Learning through example" emerged as a key theme in the online survey. While we know that modeling behavior is an effective method of communication, some respondents noted that not having had positive role models to emulate led to difficulties both in establishing healthy relationships of their own and knowing how to discuss the topic of relationships with their own children.

I recognize that the group of parents who volunteered for the online survey is diverse and not representative of all parents. Nonetheless, these parents gave helpful information to report in this book. Comments from the parents are interspersed throughout the chapters, with the heading **Relationship Advice in Action**, to demonstrate the types of messages parents choose to discuss with their children (or not). The comments show individual views on what it means to be in a good relationship, what quality they'd most like in a relationship for their children, what they wish they would have learned about relationships, and other relationship thoughts and advice.

ASKING THE WHYS

As a child, I always asked the question "why?" *Why?* I've always been interested in why things are the way they are and why they work the way they do. My father is a psychiatrist, and my mother is a therapist, so I come from a therapy-oriented family, and we analyzed relationships a lot together as a family. In graduate school, I became interested in interactions when it comes to long-term relationships. And I asked again: *Why?* The "whys" of interaction, and what keeps couples together and happy and what breaks them apart.

I continue to ask those "whys." I see personally and as a researcher that relationships are critical for our health and well-being. When our relationships are going well and they're healthy and happy, we as individuals are healthier and happier in general. Physically we're healthier. But I'm always asking that question... *Why?* Why do relationships make us happy? Why do we spend so much time finding and maintaining those connections? Why are relationships so vital to us as human beings, and essential to our health and well-being in life? I'm fascinated by it all. The complexities of relationships are why I've committed my life to understanding them and their role in life.

People aren't getting good information about the reality of relationships. It's why I talk about relationships, write about relationships, and bring relationships to the public through science-based information. I understand what it takes to have an exceptional relationship. I have dedicated my life to helping others understand what it takes and how to take action to improve relationships.

This book will give you both the confidence and the messages you so desperately need to guide your children. I want to be sure that you have the knowledge and skills to have exceptional, healthy relationships because, as parents, you have the responsibility to help your children have the same. In addition, the skills and information in this book will help you build your lifelong relationship with your children. My aim is to draw from all my roles—using the groundbreaking findings from my academic research, the insights from relationship counseling and coaching, and my own family experiences—and make them accessible to you.

BREAKING IT DOWN

In this book, you'll discover positive, simple strategies to help you when talking to your children about relationships. I also provide tips to examine your own relationships and interactions with other people so that you can model and provide positive examples for your children. The themes in each of the eight chapters that follow will give you insight into the most important relationship issues and help you to confidently and competently approach them with your children.

Chapter 1, "Practice Relationships as a Priority," is about healthy relationships as a priority for you and your children. You'll learn what trust means, why it is critical to the relationship with your children, and specific strategies to build trust up in your interactions with them. You'll also discover that the leading cause of relationship failure is frustration and how to help your children set realistic relationship expectations. I'll share several "conversation starters" to examine relationship beliefs.

In Chapter 2, "Initiate Conversations about the Topics That Matter," you'll learn how to begin what are likely to be the most important conversations you will have with your young adult children. You'll need to take stock of the biases you carry around about close relationships. I also provide critical strategies to lay the groundwork for having relationship conversations, so that you'll have your children's full attention. You'll discover age-appropriate relationship topics and how to ask the right kinds of questions to guide the conversation.

The focus of Chapter 3, "Show Gratitude and Appreciation," is why expressing affirmation can make a significant difference in relationship happiness and is essential to happy, healthy relationships. When you receive affirmation, you're happier, you're more motivated to work on your relationship, and you feel better physically and psychologically. You'll learn specific ways to express gratitude, through words and actions. I'll also describe how to model gratitude with your children, provide scripts to start conversations about gratitude, and address gender differences in approaches to showing appreciation. A quiz in this chapter will reveal your children's personal preference for receiving affirmation.

Chapter 4, "Change the Way You Speak," is all about the vital topic of interpersonal communication. Understanding how different types of verbal and nonverbal communication affect the way we convey messages and receive them can fend off the types of miscommunications that can harm relationships. You will discover how to share this important information with your children in fun ways, so that they can say what they mean and better interpret what others are saying to them. You will also learn how to model and participate in these effective communication strategies with your children.

Chapter 5, "Manage the Battles: Keys to Handling Stress and Conflict," examines how to manage these inevitable facets of any close relationship. I emphasize the role you play in modeling healthy coping behaviors and describe practical tips for equipping your children with the tools to both handle stress and fight fair in conflicts. Using findings from the EYM study and other research, I describe how men and women process conflict differently and how disagreements between parents can affect a child's well-being.

Chapter 6, "Bring the Topic of Money Out into the Open," delves into the importance of having conversations about and managing money in relationships. You'll learn how to explore the meaning of money with your children and give them a "money vocabulary." Instilling financial knowledge in your children not only makes them more resourceful, but it is also proven to benefit their future relationships.

In Chapter 7, "Make a Big Deal About the Right Relationship," you will learn the top four ways for your children to meet love partners. You'll also discover that there are two kinds of love, how your children can recognize if a relationship is right for them, and if or when to include sex in their love relationship(s). The science-based information that you acquire in this chapter will help your children's relationships get off to a good start.

Chapter 8, "Handle Heartbreaks and Other Love Challenges," focuses on the most common relationship and love challenges that you might experience with your young adult children. Many parents might be facing these challenges right now. You'll learn what the love challenges are and why they are difficult. I'll also provide you with specific ways to address or deal with these love challenges that will preserve your healthy, happy relationship with your children over the long haul *and* improve your children's love relationships.

This book is designed to be fun, illuminating, and above all, easy to put into practice. I have scattered activities such as quizzes, exercises, self-assessments, stories, and question guides throughout the book to make the strategies and conversations more tangible. You'll also find references to research-based relationship tips from my EYM study, findings from other research studies, and relationship advice in action from my online parent survey. Knowing what information is scientifically proven can give you an added measure of assurance that the information you share and put into practice with your children is reliable.

Enjoy the conversations with your children that this book inspires. And, as you engage in these important conversations, rest assured that you're doing your best to fulfill that promise of helping make their lives as happy as possible. And yours too!

CHAPTER 1

Practice Good Relationships as a Priority

You already know intuitively that when you're in a happy relationship, you feel good. You feel on top of your game. Everything around you seems brighter and you are more hopeful. That's because love and relationships are the backbone of our existence as human beings. But just being "in a relationship" isn't enough; you need to be in a happy, positive relationship in order to truly get the benefits that relationships can give you.

Scores of scientific research also confirm that happy relationships have profound effects on our physical and mental health. When you are in happy, loving relationships, you are better able to handle stress, more likely to be physically active, less likely to be depressed and suffer from illnesses, and in general, you live a longer and healthier life. In fact, people without happy relationships in their lives are two to five times more likely to die sooner than those who have a sense of closeness in their lives. An 80-year Harvard University study on adult development (considered the world's longest study of adult life) found that good relationships are the factors that matter the most for long-lasting happiness—more than money or fame, social class, IQ, or even genes!

Given all of this science and research on the positive effects of good relationships, the key question is: How can you best set your children up for healthy lives, physically and mentally? Answer: **Seize the moment and make good relationships a priority for you and for them!**

In this chapter, you'll learn about *two vital ingredients to a happy, healthy relationship*, so that you can practice good relationships as a priority with your young adult child. First, Billy Joel sang about it and, boy, did he have it right. When it comes to healthy happy relationships, it's a matter of **trust**. Trust is the most important and essential aspect to develop with your child so they can share their feelings and thoughts with you, which will set the path for a lifelong relationship with your children and help your child practice trust-building for their love relationships. In the first part of this chapter, I will discuss what trust means and why it is important, and then I'll share some trust-building exercises to do with your child, along with strategies to rebuild trust after a betrayal. Further, if your child is resistant to speak with you about relationships in general, or more specifically about their own love relationships, it may be that you need to build up the trust within your relationship first. Trust assures them that they are safe and loved, regardless of the information they share with you. The trust-building exercises I share with you in this chapter will help lay the groundwork for less challenging discussions about relationships.

Second, contrary to popular belief, the leading cause of relationship failure (of all kinds!) is not conflict, lack of communication, or incompatibility. It is frustration. Where does frustration come from? It comes from **unrealistic expectations about relationships**. Parents can help children form realistic expectations, not only about love relationships, but also relationships with friends, family, colleagues, and others. In the second part of this chapter, you'll learn what the research on relationships tells us about how partners relate, and how to mesh these facts while relaying relationship advice to your child. I will discuss the differences between relationship myths and relationship realities. As you discover ways to teach your child how to dispel and debunk relationship myths with science and facts, you will also find ways to share what a good relationship looks like, whether there are models of these relationships around them, and how a good partner should treat them. The goal is to help your child shed unrealistic expectations and replace them with more reasonable points of view. The outcome: **They'll live happier lives because they'll form healthier happier relationships.**

WHAT IS TRUST?

Trust is the most important and essential aspect of any good, happy relationship. In order for any relationship to move forward, you need to develop and nurture a level of trust. When you trust someone, you believe that person tells you the truth, won't hurt or deceive you, and has your best interests at heart. In a loving relationship, it's important that you and your partner each feel a sense of trust. This faith reduces your inhibitions and worries and allows you to reveal feelings and dreams with each other. This sharing makes you feel closer and more connected to the other person. Thus, trust is an important thing to build with your child so they can feel comfortable to share their thoughts and feelings with you—and so that they can develop it in their love relationships going forward.

In my long-term study of marriage, I asked the happiest couples to name their most important relationship expectation. A whopping 92% of the men and 96% of the women answered, "You should feel that your spouse would never hurt or deceive you." There has to be trust.

Trust-Building Exercises for You and Your Child

Here are four exercises that you can do with your child to build trust in your relationship. These exercises will not only develop trust between you, but they will help your child understand and experience what is needed to build trust in their own love relationships.

1. **Disclose Parallel Personal Information to Each Other**

   One way to build trust in a relationship is for you and your child to share personal information with each other. You can ask your child questions about past, present, or possible future experiences or thoughts: What are they most proud of doing in the last year? What do they regret not doing in the last year? What would it be like if they grew up as a child of the president (or their teacher or a rock star/reality TV star)? When your child answers these questions, and you listen with open ears, trust builds between the two of you. It is important that you also share personal information in kind after you listen to your child's answers. This may not be easy for you, but it is essential to build trust with your child. It will also model healthy, positive trust-building.

   My client Fran has a 21-year-old daughter to whom she would like to feel closer. She also knows that her daughter is dating a 28-year-old who is the father to a young child. She would like to talk to her daughter about this relationship and her feelings toward this man. She worries about her daughter's relationship with someone who is seven years older than her and who already has a child. I told Fran to write down seven personal questions on a piece of paper and put them in a large bowl (e.g., What are you most proud of doing in the last year? What is the most important quality of a good relationship? What do you hope to be doing five years from now?). She and her daughter should then sit down together, pick each piece of paper out of the bowl, and both share the answers in front of each other. This conversation might even last a few nights! The outcome: It will build trust between Fran and her daughter, it will model trust-building for her daughter in her own love relationship, and it will allow Fran to understand what her daughter is thinking and feeling in her current love relationship.

2. **Take Initiative and Reveal Without Expecting Anything in Return**
   You can also reveal personal stories and information to your child (e.g., "when I was young, Grandma and I didn't always get along with each other"; "when I was in college, I got an 'F' in my first English course"; "when your mother and I were first married, we struggled with money"), without asking questions of them. Studies show that if one person shares something personal and both people are interested in growing the relationship, then the other person naturally responds at the same level of intimacy. This may not happen immediately, but over time this can gradually build trust in the relationship. You can also use how much each of you is disclosing to each other over time as an index of whether the relationship is developing trust or not.

3. **Hold a Trust Chat**
   Another way to build trust in a relationship is to have what I call a "trust chat" with your child. This exercise is typically for those 18 years or older. Sit down and ask them questions like:

   a. "What do trust and commitment mean to you?"

b. "Is it acceptable to keep secrets from someone when you have a good relationship with them? If so, what kinds of secrets are okay?"

c. "If trust has developed, what are things that someone might do to break that trust? And if someone betrays your trust—can that trust be rebuilt? If yes, how can someone win back your trust?"

4. **Engage in Team-Building Challenges or Activities**

Trust can also develop in a relationship when you do activities together that require both of you to complete the task. Activities that are built on teamwork, like taking care of a puppy, planting flowers in a garden, or working on a puzzle, create trust. It is the process of executing successful outcomes together that builds trust and reliance on each other. Doing these activities with your child will develop trust between you and them.

Trust Challenges

Granted, trust takes time to develop. And as supportive and patient as you are, you can't make your child trust you. For some people, trusting others is challenging because they are caught emotionally in the past or afraid of being hurt. Be patient. Give it time. Keep trying. Model healthy trust-building and the notion is that even if they don't develop that trust with *you*, they will understand and learn how to build it in their love relationships over time.

Also, the trust that you and your child build up over time can be broken, if *either of you* breaks that trust, by lying, sharing secrets, breaking rules that you've set for them (e.g., curfew, expectations for behavior, etc.), or not being supportive when they expected you to be there. When someone betrays trust in some way, the trust that two people have developed over time is broken. We call these breaks in trust **betrayals**. These betrayals are painful, because you are confronted with the fact that your child (or your child is confronted with the fact that you), is not as dependable, reliable, or as honest as you thought.

But the big message here: You can regain trust after a betrayal, but it takes work, conscious effort, and commitment from you. Be patient. Give it time. Keep trying. Here are tips to help rebuild trust with your child:

1. **Offer a heartfelt apology.** A sincere apology is one where the betrayer takes responsibility for their actions. Whether your child accepts your apology (or you accept your child's apology) may depend on whether this is a one-time behavior or whether this is a consistent pattern.

2. **Discuss both people's perspectives.** Does your child have a sense of why you did what you did (or do you have a sense of why your child did what they did)? You don't need to agree on the circumstances that prompted the breaking of trust, but you do need to understand one another's feelings, motives, and expectations—especially if you want your child to trust you going forward (or you want to trust your child going forward).

3. **List the positives in your relationship.** Coming up with these qualities (either with your child or you separately) is important because focusing on the good aspects of your relationship will remind each of you that one mistake or issue doesn't determine the quality of a relationship.

4. **Seek assistance from a counselor or therapist.** When trust is broken, depending on the specific incident that broke the trust, it can be very challenging (to both you and your child) to rebuild, regardless of how strong a

relationship or person might be. It can be tough to break a consistent pattern of hurt and anger. A therapist's perspective and help can be very beneficial. You can seek help together or separately.

SETTING REALISTIC EXPECTATIONS TO NEUTRALIZE FRUSTRATION

The next important way to practice good relationships as a priority is to help your child set realistic expectations about what to look for in happy, healthy love relationships and about the realities and struggles that all romantic relationships undergo. I recommend that you work on building trust with your child first, before you move on to this next section. Once you develop trust, they will be more likely to discuss, share personal information, and take the quiz about relationships that I present later in this chapter.

When I first became a university professor almost 30 years ago, I began my first day of class by asking the students, "Who among you expects to marry or commit to a life partner one day?" All hands shot up. I have asked this question every semester since then and, surprisingly, nothing has changed. When I ask follow-up questions, the students consistently share that they expect their love partner to fulfill *all* their needs, and they expect to stay married or committed to a single partner at some point in their lives. It always surprises me how these young adults can project such lofty ideals onto relationships and be so certain of finding one person who encompasses all the qualities they need for relationship fulfillment and permanence, particularly given that my study and others find that about 46–50% of married couples end up divorced.

Most children and teens are taught that their partner or spouse should be the embodiment of everything they could wish for in a relationship. They learn that when two people find each other and commit to each other, their lives will be forever intertwined. Young people are taught to expect that their partner should be their soul mate, their best friend, an excellent parent, a great lover, a good provider, a loving caregiver, a willing volunteer, and someone who is physically fit, healthy, sensitive, generous, well-liked by their friends and family, open-minded, polite, intelligent, with similar interests, and happy to spend leisure time with them. Phew! No love partner can fulfill all these expectations. People who believe that a romantic partner should have every one of these traits have unrealistic ideals. And, when nothing short of perfection is the standard of measurement, frustration inevitably sets in and unhappiness results.

Frustration stems from unmet expectations. If you expect that a relationship *should* develop or unfold in one way (or that a partner *should* treat you a certain way), and it doesn't happen that way, frustration creeps in. In such instances, the reality of the relationship doesn't match the expectations of what you've learned about how a relationship (or relationship partner) *should* be. People walk around with a lot of "should statements" in their heads: My friends *should* know what kind of support I need; my family *should* want to spend time with my romantic partner; my romantic partner *should* be able to read my mind. Most of the time, these "should statements" are unrealistic assumptions or expectations, which create frustration and disappointment because they're not supported in real life.

Frustration is tension that can build until it eventually erupts into anger and disappointment. It eats away at the happiness in a relationship. Inevitably, relationships will undergo some degree of frustration over their lifespan. I know mine have. When I first became a mother, I expected that my children would bond more with me than my husband. I had been conditioned to believe the myth that children *should* always want their mothers more than their fathers, regardless of situations, age, or gender. As a result, I was devastated when my daughter's first word was "Daddy," not "Mommy." And when my daughter, at age two, said she wanted only her father to read her a bedtime story (for almost two months), I seriously contemplated quitting my job to stay home 24/7. It wasn't until I met other mothers in a toddler playgroup who had similar experiences that my frustration eased, and I changed my expectations. Finding other mothers who were experiencing the same parent-child dynamic made me less disappointed and helped prepare me for the same situation when it happened with my son three years later.

Children and teens learn about love and relationships through family, friends, and social norms around them. They are continually exposed to relationship misinformation perpetuated through media and our myth-laden society—including which parent a baby will bond with. As I mentioned in the Introduction, children are influenced by their family life, by how you interact with them and handle stress, and by observing the ups and downs in friends' and other family members' relationships. They watch and they listen. But the truth is, most of what they learn about how romantic relationships "should be" is not backed by facts, research, or science. They are unaware of the barrage of relationship misinformation influencing them and setting them up for unnecessary frustration and disappointment.

Further compounding the problem is the fact that adults tend to perpetuate unrealistic relationship expectations by shielding young people from the conflicts that are a natural byproduct of any close relationship. Many parents, for example, won't have disagreements in front of their children, believing they should always appear congenial. But, when children aren't exposed to conflict and effective ways to work through it, they don't understand that clashes and arguments are an inevitable part of all romantic relationships. Then, when children grow up and have their own love relationships, they're unprepared when disagreements arise. They mistakenly assume that something is not right about their partner or their relationship, because they believe that happy or good relationships don't have conflict. I'll dig deeper into how to manage conflicts in Chapter 3.

Relationship Advice in Action

"I talk to my kids all the time about healthy relationships....I talk to them about the hard work any healthy relationship has—and that being mad at the person you love is part of a normal relationship. When I'm grumbly about a stupid thing their dad does, it doesn't mean I love him less."
—*relationship survey response*

HOW TO SET REALISTIC RELATIONSHIP EXPECTATIONS WITH YOUR CHILD

Helping ensure that your child has happy, healthy love relationships entails making sure they have realistic beliefs and expectations about what good love relationships look like, and how a good partner treats the other partner. Also important is helping your child learn to differentiate between common sense attitudes toward relationships that are unrealistic, and the truths or realities of happy, healthy relationships.

What good relationships look like—young teens (ages 13–15)

When your child is a younger teen engage them in conversations that express realistic expectations for relationships, and that share how good relationships look and feel. Conversations will focus on what family or friends do to help or support each other. Encourage your child to begin thinking about how good relationships make them feel. Do they feel comforted, cared for, supported, happy, and better off with friends and family around them? Ask your child why they like their friend, "X." Ask how they feel when their friend (or grandma, grandpa, aunt, uncle) calls them to say hi. By concentrating on what purpose their relationships serve in their lives *and* the positive emotions they experience as a result of these relationships, they begin to set realistic expectations about what feelings should come from their current and future close relationships.

Point out how people who care for each other don't always have to agree, and that every relationship has its ups and downs. When problems arise among your child's friends and family members, or in books or shows, ask your child what feelings those create, such as anger, sadness, stubbornness, loneliness, or rejection. Talk about the good times that come from your child's relationships, too, and ask what feelings come from these: excitement, happiness, joy, or feeling special. Help your child find ways to share those feelings in their relationships.

Relationship Advice in Action

"I've told [my daughter] about love and how it's not always perfect. I told her that her friendships will come and go, and nobody is perfect, nor do they have to be."
—*relationship survey response*

What good relationships look like—young adults (ages 16–28 or beyond)

When your child reaches young adulthood, conversations concerning relationship expectations become more involved as you examine in detail the myths versus realities of relationships. Young adult children (or even those in their late 20s and 30s) begin developing their own expectations for what makes up a good relationship. Make time for one-on-one conversations that give them opportunities to express their perceptions and understanding of what comprises a healthy relationship.

Relationship Advice in Action

"In response to why the topic of relationships has not been discussed yet: 'Not sure how to raise the subject and not sure they would want to hear.'" —*relationship survey response*

It can be challenging to start these conversations with your child. The four conversation starters below are useful in facilitating discussions with children (ages 16–28+ years) about what characterizes a good relationship. These conversations also help you and your child dig more deeply into personal relationship beliefs, and help you identify whether your child's expectations are realistic or not.

Before embarking on the conversation starters that follow, review them to decide which are best suited for your child's age and readiness to communicate about relationship topics. The conversations intensify sequentially, beginning with conversations more appropriate for younger children. You can use a specific situation in your child's life (e.g., first dating relationship or first breakup) or a stage of life (e.g., going off to college or moving into their first apartment) as an opportunity to start the conversations with your child. You may choose to eventually discuss all four topics with your child.

CONVERSATION STARTER #1: IMPORTANT RELATIONSHIP QUALITIES

Set aside a time when there will be no distractions to begin this conversation. For this discussion, you will have a simple and direct conversation that starts with asking short questions to gather information.

Bear in mind that the first part of this conversation requires that your child names specific relationship qualities (and requires that you *not* share your own ideas about "correct" qualities until later). Note, too, that as you start this conversation, you will not react to answers you believe are right or wrong. Try to withhold your opinion. Your focus is on getting your child to talk and share their thoughts and ideas.

Start the conversation by asking two basic questions:

1. What does a good relationship look like?

2. What qualities are important in a relationship to make you happy?

After your child lists as many qualities as they can think of (with a few prompts of "Anything else that you see as important...?"), write the list on a piece of paper. In this way, you paraphrase what your child said to you as you jot down the responses. This allows your child to hear what they said, and it also ensures that you were attentive to whatever they described to you. (I realize that writing down your child's list of "good relationship qualities" after the fact may seem counterintuitive, but while your child is talking, it is important to have eye contact and show that you are actively listening. Wait until your child is finished before taking out paper and pen to write down the traits they shared.)

After you have your child's list of "good relationship qualities" (and it doesn't matter if there are two or two dozen qualities), go over the list and ask your child *why* each specific quality is important in a happy relationship. What about each quality makes them happy? Finally, ask how they learned about the importance of that quality. Your discussion should focus on the reasons for their answers, why the qualities are important, and where they learned about the importance of these qualities in a relationship.

Only at this point in the conversation will you offer your own opinions about how a healthy relationship looks. If needed, you can discuss realistic versus unrealistic expectations, and how depictions of good relationships in TV shows, movies, or even among a friend's parents may not be the most realistic portrayal of good relationships. The two of you can discuss ideas about where to find better examples (e.g., *Psychology Today*'s list of blogs on relationships, found at https://www.psychologytoday.com/us/blog/index) or more accurate information about what qualities make up a good relationship (discussed further in the next section).

> ### Relationship Advice in Action
>
> "I discussed how important it is to treat people you love well." —*relationship survey response*

CONVERSATION STARTER #2: ELEVEN BUILDING BLOCKS OF HAPPY LOVE RELATIONSHIPS

Research shows that healthy intimate relationships—**both romantic and between family members and friends**—*share 10 similar qualities*. These 10 qualities are considered the building blocks of happy relationships.[2] The couples who have been the happiest in my Early Years of Marriage long-term study also mentioned these qualities as among those they considered important to their relationships over time. And, from gathering research on couples for more than 30 years, I've found that the 10 qualities are indeed predictive of relationship happiness. You will note that I have added an 11th quality, considered important for happy romantic love relationships, although not a quality of happy intimate relationships that are between family members or friends.

For this discussion, take each of the 11 qualities of healthy intimate love relationships that follow and have a conversation with your child that focuses on these questions:

1. Do they know what each word means and are they able to define each quality? How does each quality get expressed in a relationship?

2. Can they identify whether a relationship (or partner) exhibits that particular quality?

3. Do they know couples that model any of the 11 qualities in their relationship?

The 11 qualities and their definitions follow. Compare your child's understanding of each quality with the definition provided. They may not fully understand what a certain quality means (which is to be expected—I would be surprised if anyone could correctly identify all the terms below!). Describe what the definitions mean and how to identify whether a relationship (or partner) embodies each particular quality.

Eleven Proven Qualities of Healthy Love Relationships

1. **Knowledge:** Intimate partners share extensive personal, often confidential, information with each other.

2. **Caring:** Intimate partners feel more affection for one another than they do for most others.

3. **Interdependence:** Intimate partners' lives are intertwined, and they have strong, diverse, and enduring influence on each other.

4. **Mutuality:** Intimate partners think of themselves as a couple instead of as two entirely separate individuals. Their lives overlap.

5. **Trust:** Intimate partners expect treatment from one another that is fair, honorable, not harmful, and responsive to their needs.

6. **Commitment:** Intimate partners expect their relationship to continue, and they work to realize that goal.

7. **Respect:** Intimate partners admire each other, think highly of each other, and treat each other with consideration and compassion.

8. **Social Support:** Intimate partners rely on each other to help them through difficulties. They also provide help and encouragement to each other.

9. **Share Good News:** Intimate partners celebrate the good times with each other and are pleased by each other's successes.

10. **Affirmation:** Intimate partners make each other feel valued, understood, special, and cared for, through words or actions.

11. **Sexuality:** When two intimate partners are in a romantic love relationship, this relationship often has a sexual component. Sex is a group of behaviors, actions, and experiences that may include, but are not restricted to, kissing, oral sex, anal sex, touching a partner's body, or sexual intercourse. Healthy sexual behaviors for couples are consensual and nonexploitative.

Use this conversation starter and list of relationship qualities to create teaching moments with your child. The goal is to *teach* them about realistic (and scientifically proven) qualities that lead to healthy relationships. I also encourage you to address how these "realities about relationships" (developed through scientific research), are a reliable reference for their personal relationship experiences in the future.

As mentioned above, one of the qualities of a romantic love relationship is a sexual component. The topic of sex and relationships will be addressed further in Chapter 7, "Make a Big Deal about the Right Relationship." A full discussion of how to talk about sex, contraception, and STIs (sexually transmitted infections) with your young adult child is beyond the scope of this particular book, but there are other resources available (see, for example, *Ten Talks Parents Must Have with Their Children About Sex and Character* by Pepper Schwartz and Dominic Cappello). To get the latest information on sexual health, you can turn to sites such as WebMD or MayoClinic.com for good information on STIs and how they are spread. Also, your child can discuss STIs and contraception with their physician, since doctors don't always discuss sex-related health issues unless they are prompted.

I recognize that families have different values and approaches to the topic of sexuality. You want to share those values with your young adult children. I support you, and this book is not intended to change those values. In the next two paragraphs, I merely present some science-based information (not values or approaches) about sexuality and young adults, so you are equipped and prepared for discussions.

First, according to the Guttmacher Institute,[3] 65% of 18-year-olds and 93% of 25-year-olds have had sexual intercourse. In addition, although your child might assume otherwise, most adolescents use contraceptives at both first sex and most recent sex (89% of females, 94% of males), with the condom being the contraceptive method most commonly used.

Second, there are hundreds of reasons why your young adult child might have sex. The most common reasons are positively oriented (e.g., love, attraction, pleasure), but some are more negative (e.g., "I wanted to impress my friends," "I didn't want my partner to leave me"). Studies[4] show that there are four overriding themes underlying these reasons for having sex. First, young adults have sex because of the emotional component; they want to express love, affection, emotional closeness, or commitment through physical intimacy. Second, young adults want to experience physical pleasure or are motivated by the physical attractiveness of their partner. The third category involves pragmatic reasons. They wish to attain some goal or outcome that is associated with sex, such as the desire to have a child, make someone jealous, or think of themselves as an adult. Finally, young adults might have sex because they are insecure, don't like their bodies, or want to keep a partner from leaving them. The assumption underlying this latter set of reasons is that sex will somehow make them feel better about themselves or the relationship.

CONVERSATION STARTER #3: SIXTEEN MOST COMMON ROMANTIC RELATIONSHIP EXPECTATIONS

The 16 most common relationship expectations reported among the 373 romantic couples in my long-term study provide an interesting focus for a conversation. As your child enters adolescence, they will begin to explore romantic relationships. This is an exercise to start your child communicating about what they think is important in a romantic relationship and how each of the following relationship expectations ranks against the others. Again, note that as you start this conversation, you will not react to answers you believe are right or wrong. Try to withhold your opinion. Your focus is on getting your child to talk and share their thoughts and ideas.

On a piece of paper (or you can do this verbally), have your child rank the importance of each expectation as it relates to their ideal of a happy relationship. Ask them to use a scale of 1 to 4:

> 1 = very important to a happy relationship
> 2 = fairly important to a happy relationship
> 3 = not very important to a happy relationship
> 4 = not at all important to a happy relationship

I conducted this exercise with all the couples in my long-term study. Each ranked the 16 expectations individually, and then discussed their answers with their partner.

Then, use your child's rankings as a launching pad for a discussion. Ask:

1. Why did you rank the statement as important or not important?

2. Where did you learn about this statement (or saw a couple with this quality)?

3. Do you think it is realistic to expect the statement to be true for a happy love relationship?

4. Since not every relationship has all 16 traits, which two are the most important? Which two are the least important?

16 Most Common Relationship Expectations

1. You should cool off before you say too much if you're fighting.

2. You should enjoy leisure time together.

3. You should control the way you express anger with each other.

4. You should each have an equal say in all important matters.

5. You should feel that your partner would never hurt or deceive you.

6. You should be ready and willing to compromise when you disagree.

7. You should have some private time away from each other.

8. You should be allowed to keep some of your money separate.

9. You should always say what is on your mind.

10. You should always settle a fight quickly.

11. You should try not to criticize your partner.

12. You should share equally in the household chores.

13. You should know the people your partner spends leisure time with.

14. You should listen carefully to one another's point of view.

15. You should take time for your own individual friends.

16. You should take the time to understand each other's sexual needs.

DID YOU KNOW? Early Years of Marriage Study Findings

For the happily married couples in my long-term EYM study, the expectation considered most important (of the 16 most common relationship expectations) was: "You should feel that your partner would never hurt or deceive you" (ranked first by 92% of men and 96% of women). This statement is all about the expectation of trust in a love relationship and I mentioned these statistics earlier in the chapter when we discussed the topic of trust. The second-most important relationship expectation for these happy couples was: "You should listen carefully to one another's point of view." Overall, men and women provided similar answers regarding which personal expectations were among the most important to their marriages.

CONVERSATION STARTER #4: UNCOVERING THE MYTHS ABOUT RELATIONSHIP EXPECTATIONS

Guiding your child's understanding of the *unrealistic* notions or myths surrounding relationships perpetuated through both the media and society will help them form more realistic expectations for their own relationships. Children are bombarded by misconceptions about love and marriage that are represented as fact yet are firmly rooted in fiction. Earlier in this chapter I described how these misconceptions can lead to frustration in their own love relationships. In contrast, research conducted with large, diverse groups of people on relationships provides data about which beliefs are considered realistic. Forming relationships around realistic expectations will help your child avoid the potential frustrations that can negatively affect their love relationships and their happiness.

The following exercise is designed to reduce potential relationship frustrations by examining which common expectations concerning the opposite sex, love, and relationships are based on myths—and are therefore unrealistic—and which ones match up with scientific findings. Knowing the facts about relationships will lead your child to reconsider their expectations and take a more realistic approach toward their relationships.

Use the short Relationship IQ Quiz that follows to start the discussion. It's a useful way to learn how much your child really knows about relationships so you can help them to expose relationship myths. Ask your child to answer each question. Then, taking each response, explore with them the scientifically based facts relating to each myth. Answers to each question, along with a short explanation, follow the quiz. Remember, each time you break down an assumption or myth-based belief, you allow your child to form more realistic expectations about relationships, which leads to happier and healthier love relationships. And just as a side note: I've been giving multiple versions of this Relationship IQ Quiz to thousands of people in the last several decades at various workshops, presentations, and seminars, and most people don't get all the answers correct.

QUIZ: Relationship IQ Quiz

For each statement, circle True or False to best describe your belief. Then, score your responses at the end.

1. True/False: You should never go to bed mad at a romantic partner.

2. True/False: Jealousy is a sign of true love and caring.

3. True/False: Women have more romantic notions and beliefs than men.

4. True/False: Early in a romantic relationship, we can see our partner for who they really are.

5. True/False: The best relationships (of all kinds) are ones with no conflict.

6. True/False: Not only do opposites attract, they're more likely to stay together over the long haul.

Scoring: The correct answer to all of the statements is "False." Give yourself one point for each correct response. Add up your points. Scores range from zero to six. The lower the score, the more your knowledge is based on myths rather than research-based realities.

And now here's the truth about relationships.

Relationship IQ question #1: You should never go to bed mad at a romantic partner. **False!**

> Many of us have been taught this by our parents or from TV shows or movies. It is a widespread myth that many people repeat. At a wedding shower I attended recently, the guests were asked to bring a note card with one piece of marital advice for the bride. Nearly one-third of the guests' cards read: "Never go to bed angry." But research tells us that solving problems when you are upset and emotional is nearly impossible. After anger flares up, the brain needs at least 30 minutes to return to normal functioning. After you calm down and get a good night's sleep, you are much more likely to see things in a new light.

Relationship IQ question #2: Jealousy is a sign of true love and caring. **False!**

> Jealousy shown by a partner or friend is not a sign of how much that person cares about you. It has more to do with insecurity than love. Jealousy and possessiveness usually stem from fear and low self-esteem. Contrary to popular belief, research shows that men and women do not differ in their tendency toward experiencing jealousy. Yet, men and women respond differently to the experience of jealousy. When men experience jealousy, they feel angry and hurt, and are more likely to retaliate, express anger, or consider

leaving. In contrast, women often respond to jealousy by trying to overcompensate to preserve the relationship. Both responses can be damaging to a romantic relationship.

Relationship IQ question #3: Women have more romantic notions and beliefs than men. **False!**

Science tells us it is actually the opposite. Studies show that men, not women, have more romanticized beliefs about love and relationships. This fact is always shocking to people. It turns out that men are more likely to believe in love at first sight, that love conquers all, and that love is necessary before commitment. Research also shows that men fall in love more quickly than women. Women are more selective and cautious about who they choose to love. Men are the romantics, not women!

Relationship IQ question #4: Early in a romantic relationship, we can see our partner for who they really are. **False!**

At the beginning of a relationship, you idealize and glorify your partner. You see them through rose-colored glasses. You ignore or minimize that person's faults or any undesirable traits that aren't flattering. Passionate love and romance are enhanced by these glorifications of your partner. Only after some time goes by do the rose-colored glasses come off, allowing you to see the imperfections that every partner—and every person—has.

Relationship IQ question #5: The best relationships (of all kinds) are ones with no conflict. **False!**

Although it might sound impressive to say, "We never fight," in both romantic relationships and friendships, the reality is that you need to occasionally disagree. Otherwise, you and your partner/friend may not be talking about important issues. A lack of conflict means you aren't really dealing with things that matter. Any two individuals with different backgrounds, families, opinions, and pursuits will inevitably disagree at some point in their relationship. Expecting no conflict is unrealistic. It is how you handle or manage the conflict that determines its effect on your relationship. I discuss more about conflict in relationships and describe effective ways to manage disagreements in Chapter 5.

Relationship IQ question #6: Opposites attract and stay together. **False!**

People are often attracted to their opposite. This is because we are naturally curious about those who are different from us. But this attraction doesn't hold up over the long term. My own research and that of others shows that *similarities in key life values*—or shared beliefs—are what keep people together and lead to happy, healthy love partnerships. It is fine to have different interests, hobbies, movie preferences, or food aversions, but those couples who share similar key life values, such as the importance of family or religion, or agree on how children should be taught and cared for, are what really help two people get along.

Relationship Advice in Action

"[The relationship topic that I have discussed with my children is] We talk about love—real love, not the love-at-first-sight notion of love..." —*relationship survey response*

REVIEWING THE STRATEGIES: HOW TO PRACTICE MAKING GOOD RELATIONSHIPS A PRIORITY

Good relationships are essential for your child's health and well-being. By making good relationships a priority with your child, you can help them live a healthier and better life. There are two important ingredients to a good love relationship to prioritize: **trust** and **realistic expectations about love relationships**. By developing trust, your child will share their feelings and thoughts with you, which will create a lifelong relationship and help them build trust in their own love relationships. In addition, parents are the best defense against the surge of misinformation that floods children's daily lives, making them vulnerable to groundless assumptions and potential frustration in their relationships. Point out the natural imperfections and rocky moments that all relationships experience, while helping them recognize the joy and warmth that make close relationships worthwhile. Draw out their emerging beliefs about the qualities that make up a happy, healthy relationship, and gently guide them away from misconceptions. Using research-based evidence, you can help them **unmask the myths** that mislead so many people into forming mistaken impressions of how good relationships will look and feel.

Strategies recap

What is Trust and Why It is Important?

- How to build trust with your child through different strategies
- How to regain trust if it breaks

Frustration and Unrealistic Relationship Expectations

- Consider when "should statements" refer to unrealistic assumptions or expectations, and how they can result in frustration and disappointment.

- Point out that conflict and disagreements are a natural part of all relationships, and that people can work through their differences without damaging their feelings for one another.

- Help younger teens explore the feelings behind both the good sides and difficult sides of relationships, and how to appropriately express those feelings.

- Use a variety of "Conversation Starters" to encourage young adults to examine their own relationship beliefs and those promoted by media and society—and learn which hold up to scientific research.

CHAPTER 2

Initiate the Conversations about the Topics that Matter

In today's multimedia, information-packed world, advice about what drives or destroys interpersonal relationships is abundant. People are privy to the ups and downs of both real and fictitious characters—especially played out in reality TV, TikTok, or Instagram, and online advice columns and gossip magazines. It has become a public pastime to voice opinions about who is relationship-worthy and who is to blame in a breakup. And, of course, everyone beyond the age of, let's say, eight, has learned a thing or two about relationships firsthand. Okay, maybe not *just* a thing or two.

As a parent over the years, you've gathered a treasure trove of information and developed many opinions about what it takes to have good relationships—or not. And now that you have a young adult child entering or already in the world of love relationships, you naturally want to share and reveal those pearls of relationship wisdom with them. You want the best for your child, so it is important to you to impart all that knowledge to them. I know it is for me!

But before you can have those important conversations with your child, it is essential to understand and identify *how to start those conversations*. In other words, you need to lay the groundwork before having the actual relationship discussions. What is the best situation or place, and what is the best way to open the discussion? Do you ask the questions, let them come to you first with questions, or just tell them the information whether they ask or not? Contrary to popular belief, it often isn't *what* you say that influences your child, but *how* you say it that matters! And it is vital to recognize that there are multiple ways to share important information, and to realize that the best method for your child when imparting the information will influence the message they hear and remember. By making sure your foundation is sound before embarking on the actual conversations, your parent-child talks will be more positive and meaningful.

In the last chapter, you learned that building trust with your child and helping them set realistic expectations about what good relationships look like are vital steps to happy, healthy love relationships. The next important step along the road is to make sure you use effective communication techniques, which includes ensuring your child feels understood, because these tools are critical to what your child learns from your conversations. If you want your child to *hear the message* behind what you're saying, it is very important that you *send clear messages* so they won't misinterpret what you say. In this chapter, I will share with you **a step-by-step approach to the best ways to start the important conversations** about relationships with your young adult children. And again, although this book is specifically geared for parents who have young adult children 16–28 years old, this approach is effective no matter what the age of your child. You'll learn to:

1. Unpack your own emotional baggage.

2. Find the right time or place to have the conversations.

3. Give consideration to your child's age, maturity, and gender.

4. Ask the right questions to initiate meaning discussions.

I present research-based steps and information, along with personal experiences from my friends, clients, and my own family.

STEP 1: LET GO OF YOUR OWN PERSONAL EMOTIONAL BAGGAGE

Before beginning these conversations about relationships, think about your ties to your own past relationships.

- Do you have strong or painful memories of your parents, family, or previous relationships?

- Are you still angry about being bullied or excluded from cliques in middle or high school?

- Did you feel a lack of acceptance or support by an ex-spouse or a former partner that still bothers you to this day?

If you answered "yes" to any of these questions, it is critical to recognize that you might be dragging these memories and feelings around with you every day (even if not consciously), and they might be affecting your child and how they view and experience relationships—romantic, platonic, and familial. It's also influencing your path for a long-term healthy, happy relationship with your child.

Take, for instance, my client Jamie. She is still furious that her father was never there during her childhood. She often rants about how he drank too much, worked too late, and never seemed to care about what she was doing or the events in her life. She also has no problem letting other people know that she sees her father's actions as the cause of her parents' divorce, or at least her mother's unhappiness. Even though she may not intend to project these negative feelings about men who drink or work long hours onto her children, it happens anyway. And when it does, her children begin to view men, or at least fathers who work a lot or drink (at all), as bad for relationship happiness and stability.

We all carry baggage

Everyone has emotional baggage. Emotional baggage is any strong emotion from your past—either positive or negative—that prevents you from being fully present now. You can hang onto these emotions so intensely that you become handcuffed by the past and it causes all sorts of issues in the present. It can affect how you compare the present to the past; how you discuss specific plots in movies, television, and books; and how you view your child's experiences and situations in school, with friends, or with romantic partners.

No two people carry the same kind of baggage. It's just like what you see at an airport. Some people whisk through the airport with sleek and lightweight carry-ons. They have baggage, but it doesn't weigh them down. Others lug a heavy bag bursting at the seams that barely fits into the overhead compartment. Sometimes, passengers are stopped at the gate because their bags are simply too big to take onto the plane. And, amazingly, some carry very little emotional baggage at all, and can somehow get by with just a briefcase or a small purse on a long flight.

When the emotional baggage connected to the past is intense or heavy and you don't work through or tackle these feelings head-on—neutralizing your attachment to the past—it will inevitably affect your child and their outlook on relationships. For example, a husband from my EYM study, Alex, has an ex-wife who had an affair while they were married. For most of the marriage (before their divorce) he was depressed and lacked confidence in himself. After the divorce—even a decade later—he wasn't angry, but the mere mention of her name would put him into a funk that lasted for weeks. His inability to trust others became a problem in all his relationships.

Alex's intense feelings connected to his ex-wife, and his lack of trust, would leak out when watching a movie or TV show with his son. He would tell his son that trust is the most vital issue in a relationship and if he didn't pick a girl who could be loyal to him, he was definitely in for a hard time. Although trust is an essential ingredient to a healthy, happy relationship, Alex's son may grow up assuming that no one (no love partner) could ever be loyal enough for a good relationship. Or he might think that it is exclusively the responsibility of the other love partner to build trust in a relationship. As you learned in Chapter 1, trust is always a two-way street and **both** partners need to work to establish and create trust.

Relationship Advice in Action

"I grew up in a somewhat weird family. Both my parents were family-oriented and had very good intergenerational relations. What kept my parents together is one of life's biggest mysteries to me. They came from quite different backgrounds and, although they didn't overtly fight a lot, there seemed to be endless tension between them. I have always looked at their marriage as a very unsuccessful one....Four of their five children got married, [and] none of us had more than one child. Somehow I got the feeling that our family of origin's experiences left us cautious about marriage and parenting." —*relationship survey response*

Unresolved issues or emotional baggage don't even have to be initiated by previous relationships. They also can arise from what you couldn't do, wanted to do, or didn't get to do in your past. For example, I wanted to be a professional tennis player in high school. I used to dream about playing tennis on the ASTA circuit, becoming a professional tennis coach at a tennis club, and traveling to play in Wimbledon or the French Open. I didn't get to live this dream (and now, I can't even imagine how I would have accomplished it or why I wanted that lifestyle). But when my children were young and playing Little League baseball and soccer, I regularly talked to them about the significance of initiating and maintaining friendships on their teams. These topics outweighed any discussions about how they played or what skills they were learning. My emotional baggage was connected to feeling as if I spent too much time during my childhood trying to excel at sports and not enough time building and developing friendships.

Take your emotional temperature

Whatever emotional baggage you have connected to the past, it is vital to unpack some of these feelings, particularly if they are intense. You want to ask yourself why they are still present and how they are affecting aspects of your current life. To do that, take your "emotional temperature." In other words, when you think about your past with an ex-partner, friend, or family member, what effect do those thoughts have on your emotions or physical well-being?

If you have unusually positive feelings, memories, and associations to a relationship in your past, you may be over-romanticizing the relationship. Conversely, if you have unusually negative responses to the past, you can usually feel these in your body in the form of tensing up, frowning, or feeling sick in your gut. A high emotional temperature is not good for you; it needs attention and healing. Once you're able to feel detached or feel very little distress toward the past or a specific person, you'll be more mentally and emotionally prepared to pass along relationship wisdom to your child. Take your emotional temperature to find out how much personal emotional baggage you need to unpack by asking yourself the 10 questions in the quiz that follows.

QUIZ: How Heavy Is Your Emotional Baggage?

How much emotional baggage do you need to unpack before you sit down with your child to discuss relationships? This is vital to find out. Start by asking yourself these true or false questions:

Parent-child relationships

1. True/False: I have fond memories of my childhood with each parent.

2. True/False: I have/had good relationships with both of my parents.

3. True/False: I feel/felt supported by my parents.

Past/current romantic relationships

4. True/False: I have never been betrayed by a romantic partner.

5. True/False: I have never been in an abusive relationship.

6. True/False: I think men/women are basically good people.

7. True/False: I feel positive about my current and past relationships.

Childhood relationships

8. True/False: I remember my childhood friendships as happy.

9. True/False: I was never bullied, excluded from cliques, or embarrassed by my friends.

10. True/False: I keep in contact with childhood friends.

Scoring: Give yourself one point for each "False" answer, then add up your score:

8–10   Your emotional baggage is so heavy you'll need to hit the gym to be able to carry it around. Despite your best efforts, your attachment to the past will have a serious effect on your relationship discussions with your child. Learn about some ways to let go of the past (below) so that your past wounds and regrets don't spill out on your child.

5–7   You still have strong feelings connected to your past. You'll need to buy a bigger carry-on because your bag is far too small for you to cram in any more emotions. Keep reading to learn about the strategies you can use to unpack the past and lighten your load.

1–4   Although your emotional baggage may seem manageable, it is still heavy. You may not recognize the strong ties that still bind you to the past. It's important to let go of your past and live in the present. I encourage you to try some of the ways to let go of your personal baggage presented below.

0   What emotional baggage? You're in a great place to discuss relationships with your child but keep reading the simple tips that follow to keep your emotional baggage light if unwanted feelings about the past creep into the present.

Let go of your own personal emotional baggage! Here are three ways to keep strong feelings about the past from sabotaging what you share about relationships with your child:

1. **Find positive ways to release intense emotions.**

   Some constructive, positive ways to release emotions associated with the past include:

   - Vigorous physical activity

   - Staying active and busy with friends and family

   - Doing volunteer service that takes you out of your self-absorption

   - Engaging in creative activities that allow you to express yourself

   - Screaming your anger and frustration in a safe place, like your car

   - Hitting and kicking a mattress

   - Taking a salsa (or any) dance class for several consecutive weeks

   - Journaling about these emotions daily until you perceive that your attitude has improved

2. **Write a really honest letter to your ex-partner, family member, or friend.**

   Another way to unpack those negative emotions is to try writing a letter to your ex-partner, friend, or family member expressing your feelings without holding back—let loose and really give that person a piece of your mind or clear the air and confess the mistakes you made in the relationship. When you're done, put the letter away. **Don't send it**. That's right; save it. This letter is for *you*. Write a letter like this once a week or once a month and keep it in a special place where no one else will find it. You can describe your anger, sadness, frustration, guilt, or other emotions. Putting your feelings on paper will help to defuse your emotions and reviewing your letters over time will allow you to see the change in yourself, and how you're putting the past behind you. *Do not send any of these letters.* Regardless of how great you think your letters are, they are for your eyes only.

3. **Don't go it alone.**

Ask for help. Read a self-help book. Seek out the advice of trusted friends and family members who you know won't mind lending you their shoulder and their ear. Rehearse your story about what happened in the past and then share it with a close other. Talking about how and why something happened in the past allows you to make sense of what occurred—and it will justify your feelings, which will help you to move on. When you share your story with friends and family, discuss what took place and your feelings about it. Concentrate on telling *your* version of the story. In addition, it is just as significant to seek out the company of good friends and family. Get outside and enjoy activities with others. If you're feeling really distressed, see a therapist or counselor. A compassionate, neutral perspective can really help.

STEP 2: PICK THE RIGHT TIME AND SITUATION

Next among the important factors to think about before beginning a conversation about relationships with your child is the situation or timing of the conversation. These are key to what your child will hear and learn and are true for *all* children, regardless of age or gender.

When anyone is hungry, tired, or thinking intensely about something else (or distracted by the television, cell phone, computer, or another person in the room), the conversation needs to wait. Your child won't be able to concentrate, process information, or hear clearly what you have to say. When you bring up relationships with your child, even if it isn't consciously perceived as critical, the discussion should take place when they are most ready and able to hear what you have to say.

Consider what distractions may get in the way before starting any conversation about relationships with your child. Ask yourself:

1. Are they just walking in from school or work?

2. Are they hungry or tired? Did you just call and wake them up from a nap?

3. Do they have the time to talk to you? (Do they only have 10 minutes to shower, eat, and get dressed before work? Is their favorite television program starting in a few minutes? Do they have a final exam tomorrow and are worried about having time to study all the material?)

4. Is this one-on-one alone time (no friends, other parent, or family members in the room, nearby, or expected to walk in)?

If any of these kinds of distractions are present, you will want to postpone your conversation until a better time. Picking the right time and situation to start these conversations will make the difference between having an attentive listener and an annoyed or unwilling listener.

Make sure you have chosen the right time and situation to start a relationship conversation. Set the stage by inviting your child out for a meal, just the two of you. Or better yet, set aside a special time and ask your child to select the activity. If you let your child choose the activity, you often have better results because they now share a stake in the time spent together. It is preferable to plan an experience together that is new and out of the ordinary so that expectations are not preset, and you can build in time to have a serious conversation.

If your child lives at home with you, informally scheduling a few moments of togetherness every day, such as walking the dog, sharing a chore, or watching a favorite television show together, also gives you regular time to connect and gradually bring up relationship topics. The easiest way to converge at least once each day is to have dinner together. If dinner is too difficult because of work or activity schedules, make a point of being together regularly at breakfast or bedtime. If you live apart, you can try to call or FaceTime to connect regularly.

One father I know called his son every night and told him exciting and exotic stories about growing up in Ghana. His stories initiated some good discussions about how he was raised, the personal values he learned from his childhood, and what it means to be a good friend or relationship partner. Even though they lived in different states, the father and son remained very close and had scheduled time each day to talk that included having meaningful discussions on important relationship topics.

Relationship Advice in Action

"We have very open communication in our family and with our children about relationships. We discuss the importance of finding a relationship that is give and take, and that communication is key. We also discuss how relationships can look different (such as same-sex), but the elements to look for are the same." —*relationship survey response*

Open communication channels

The idea is to have at least 5 to 10 minutes of conversation time regularly, and to "check in" with children, even when they are young adults. One of the traditions I started with my children when they were five or six years old and continued until they were in college and living on their own, was to ask them during dinnertime to each share the "best" and "not so best" thing that happened to them that day. We went around the table and everyone would get a chance to describe what took place during their day. This wasn't a private one-on-one conversation, but it allowed us all as a family (or whoever was available to eat dinner together that night) to connect and check in with each other. Even now, with my children living on their own, I often text them at night: "What was the best and not-so-best of your day today?"

Our family check-in time also gave me information about what was happening with teachers, friends, other students, and the people my children interacted with on a regular basis. As each person took a turn, I listened, validated the good and bad (I didn't dismiss or say they couldn't feel that negative emotion), asked a few questions if needed, and processed the information for a later time. For example, when my daughter mentioned feeling left out when a group of her friends made after-school plans without her, I filed the story away to use later when discussing how being a good friend means looking out for your friends' feelings and including them if they feel excluded. And when my teen-age son described how hard his friend's breakup with his girlfriend was hitting the friend, I knew I'd have a good example to use when I shared with him how intense emotions can be and how important it is to choose wisely before entering a romantic relationship.

Regular give-and-take conversations, like our dinnertime check-ins, lay the groundwork for open communication between parent and child. Children will know that what every family member has to say is considered relevant. They will become used to hearing one another out and to giving their attention to a family discussion. When this kind of give-and-take communication is engrained in the family culture, children don't feel blindsided when parents want to sit down and have a serious conversation about important relationship issues.

> **Relationship Advice in Action**
>
> "I would like to keep an open dialogue regarding emotions and help [my son] to build coping mechanisms that work best for his personality/interests." —*relationship survey response*

STEP 3: CONSIDER THE AGE, GENDER, AND MATURITY OF YOUR CHILD

Another crucial factor to think about before you begin a conversation about relationships is the biological age, gender, and maturity of your child. You need to ask age-appropriate questions and raise age-appropriate topics.

Developmental considerations

Social psychologists maintain that children develop the ability to infer thoughts and expectations of others between the ages of four and six. When children are young, they first begin to take cues from their parents and immediate family. Later on, as they enter school or interact in groups, they gradually become attuned to the feelings and wishes of their teachers, classmates, and playmates. This inferential ability allows them to engage in *role taking*—the process by which children differentiate other people as separate from them, imaginatively occupy the position of those others, and take/interpret their perspective. Children learn to incorporate the others' perspectives into how they view themselves, and then into how their actions are connected to another's thoughts, feelings, and perceptions. According to George Herbert Mead,[5] a distinguished social psychologist in the early 1900s, at first children take the roles of others one at a time (grandmother, teacher, mother, mail carrier, etc.). The next stage evolves as children begin to differentiate and imagine the perspectives or viewpoints of several others, and of societal standards, at the same time.

As children grow older and participate in regular organized activities or playgroups, they begin to develop what we call a "generalized other"—when children imagine what is expected of them as they participate in specific groups, positions, or relationships. They learn these expectations by watching and observing how other people respond to them when they are in these different positions or roles. Their awareness of a *generalized other* helps children infer societal demands and standards given different roles and relationships, and to incorporate these societal standards into their own personal attitudes and behaviors. A good example of this awareness, later on, might be if your child was at a college party where many people were drinking alcohol. As the night progressed and one friend grabbed their car keys to drive home (after having too many drinks), your child might imagine what is expected of them in this situation as a good friend (i.e., given how friends treated them in similar situations, observing your behavior in similar situations, or learning information in college workshops) and encourage the friend to call an Uber or Lyft instead of driving home drunk. As children develop a notion of societal standards and expectations, parents can begin to ask questions about relationships that facilitate their recognition of the implications or consequences of their actions. These questions allow children to look at the outcomes of their actions (and of others' actions), given the generalized expectations of others.

Questions to ask that can broaden a child's awareness of social standards and expectations about relationships can take the form of prompts, such as:

- If a friend tells you a secret or something private, what do you do with that information?

- What feels worse: when a person only pretends to like you, or when someone tells you to your face that they don't want to be friends?

- How do you think your friends would treat you if you started being friends with someone outside your group?

- What do you think loyalty has to do with friendship?

Turn to Disney movies for relationship conversation-starters

You've watched them, your child has watched them, and your parents may have watched them, too. Disney movies are ageless and well loved. *Even teenage and young adult children can still enjoy watching them.* But, as adults, we recognize outdated stereotypes in some of our old favorites: women needing to be rescued by men, romanticized male-female relationships, body types representing good or evil, and a heterosexist worldview, to name a few issues.

One study by linguists Carmen Fought and Karen Eisenhauser, as reported in the *Washington Post*,[6] analyzed all the dialogue in Disney movies. They found that in the classic three Disney Princess films, women spoke as much as, or more than, men (*Snow White* 50-50; *Cinderella* 60-40; *Sleeping Beauty* 71-29). But the researchers also found that in the 1990s, the Disney films changed, and princess movies began to see men speaking more than women.

They found that men speak 68% of the time in *The Little Mermaid*; 71% of the time in *Beauty and the Beast*; and 90% of the time in *Aladdin*.

Watch or rewatch the movies with your young adult child, maybe when they are home on university break or visiting for the holidays and ask about the relationships portrayed in the movies to start instructive conversations.

1. ***Beauty and the Beast***

   - Why were people so surprised that Belle loved to read a lot?

   - Why do you think Belle didn't want to marry Gaston?

   - How did the Beast treat Belle that led her to love him?

   - What do you think Belle saw in the Beast that gave her an idea of who he was inside?

2. ***The Lion King***

   - Why would Scar want to betray, and even kill, his nephew Simba?

   - What did Mufasa want Simba to remember when he looked at the stars in the sky and why was that important?

   - What would have happened if Simba had not run away after the stampede that killed his father?

   - Was Nala being a good friend when she confronted Simba about living up to his responsibilities?

3. *The Little Mermaid*

- Why did Ariel's father become so angry when he found out that she had saved Eric? (Was he just mean, or did he have a reason?)

- Could Ariel be her true self when she was on land? What changes did she have to make?

- Is it okay to change who you are and leave those who love you for someone you don't really know?

- What about Ariel is beautiful and attractive? Is Ursula beautiful and attractive?

4. *Frozen*

- Why did Elsa hide her powers from her sister Anna?

- Why was Anna willing to marry someone she'd only known for one day?

- Did Kristoff's concern for Elsa mean that he loved her?

- What did Elsa discover that allowed her to control her power?

The age of your child is important not only for the type of conversation you have, but for the specific questions you ask and how much information you reveal or share. Maturity is critical because the ability to talk about feelings and the emotions of others changes with age. It is also important to pay attention to the type of relationships your child is experiencing, because in adolescence and young adulthood, friendships and romantic relationships influence how they see, and feel about, themselves.

Children regularly compare themselves to friends, to same-gendered others, and to romantic others and base their self-esteem, sense of self, and body image on those comparisons. What are their friends doing and what kinds of relationships are they having? What do the other girls' (or boys') bodies look like? Who has a boyfriend/girlfriend and who doesn't? Pressure to fit in with what their friends are doing is a large part of this social comparison process.

Different conversations, questions, and topics work better for different ages. Cultural norms and standards also affect the conversations that are expected and accepted within the family at various ages. But even *more* critical than biological age and culture is how mature your child is in terms of interpersonal relationships, whether they have friends who are beginning to discuss various topics, and the birth order in the family. Studies show that younger siblings tend to hear more mature information and discussions about relationships from older siblings (and their friends) and the time frame for important parent-child discussions can move up. In addition, younger siblings often seek out older siblings to ask their questions about sexuality and relationships. It is better if the parent initiates conversations to try to head off (or amend) these sibling conversations.

Gender development considerations

The gender of the child is also an important factor for how and what you discuss. Although research finds that mothers are more likely to discuss sexuality and relationships with *both* daughters and sons (compared to fathers), parents in general are more likely to talk with their young adult daughters than sons. Sons would prefer to have their fathers (or male adult figures) participate in these discussions, but many adult men do not feel equipped to have these discussions.

Children's involvement in dating and romantic relationships increases notably between the ages of 12 and 18. It is common for parents at this time to share their family values and expectations concerning their child's dating and sexual behaviors. Be aware, however, whether you express gender-based attitudes and expectations for your child. Studies[7] show that there are gender differences in parental attitudes and communication toward children's dating and romantic relationships: Fathers and mothers are more restrictive and less approving of their daughters' relationships and sexuality than their sons' same behaviors. Although parents may have the best intentions, these restrictions and negative opinions can lead girls to think that their parents don't trust them. They also increase parent-child conflicts, which in turn can have adverse outcomes for girls' romantic relationships (including lack of communication, conflict, and girls' mistrust of dating partners).

When discussions about dating and sexual behavior become too negative and restrictive, children can shut down. Be aware of the need to keep a positive tone when imparting values and attitudes concerning sexual relationships. In families with children of both genders, parents should make sure they aren't giving different messages about dating and sexual behaviors to their sons and daughters.

Know your child's interpersonal style

Your child's personality also may determine whether they are ready for a specific relationship conversation and how the talk itself progresses. For example, if your child likes to process information inwardly and find a solution or resolve a question before reaching out for assistance, then it is important to let them analyze or process ideas before you continue a conversation about a topic. In this case, you may want to start with a general question, but then allow your child to step back and think about the answer or the question and get back to you. However, if your child is the type who seeks out others for advice and solutions before making decisions, then you can initiate a conversation and process it with them at that moment.

You essentially have to know your child and watch for the cues that they are ready for specific information. Children develop at different rates and they settle into a particular stage at their own speed. If you start a conversation and you perceive by your child's response that it is too much, wait. You'll have opportunities to discuss the subject later. If you start a relationship conversation and your child seems interested or they ask for further information, then it is most likely developmentally appropriate, and you can continue forward.

I vividly remember one Thanksgiving when we invited several families to our house. About 25 of us were sitting around the table eating turkey, when my daughter, who was 10 years old at the time, asked, "Mom, what is a rebound chick? And does that have anything to do with poultry?"

Of course, it would have been asking too much for the adults and older youth around the table to not respond with gasps and chuckles. Seeing the embarrassed look on my daughter's face, I asked her whether she knew what the word "rebound" meant, and had she ever heard of the slang word "chick" used for someone other than a small chicken. She quickly said no and explained that she had just heard a song on the radio called "Rebound Chick." The main course of our meal must have reminded her of the "chick" in the song she'd heard.

I looked up the lyrics to the song later that night and they essentially croon about finding a rebound relationship, not love. My daughter assumed that when someone was on the rebound, they didn't want love. But what did that mean? And was "chick" a negative word to use for a girl or woman? At that moment at the table, because all eyes were on me (and my daughter), I thought it was best to steer clear of the nuance behind the lyrics and I simply stated that "rebound" was not a bad word. It was typically used for someone who just experienced a relationship that ended, and that sometimes after a really special relationship ends with someone we love a lot, we just aren't ready to love another person again so intensely. Sometimes you're ready to love again right away, and sometimes you're not. It depends on the person and the relationship. But if you're not ready to love again, if you're still thinking about that person all the time, or you're still sad or angry and you do start a relationship, some people call that a "rebound relationship."

I wasn't sure she wanted or needed additional details or further explanation on that front yet—or at least not at the dinner table with 23 other people staring at us. But I added that "chick" was a slang term for girl, and that it was often derogatory or negative and was not an appropriate word to use for any female, at any age. It wasn't a swear word, but it was an inappropriate word.

My daughter responded with, "thank you," and I knew any further discussion on the topic would be approached at another time. Everyone else, thankfully, was also ready to move on with eating and other conversations.

For me, this situation is such a vivid memory, even though my daughter, son, husband, and friends remember nothing of it. I also remember reading the lyrics to the entire song and noting the section that my daughter didn't bring up or mention (about the places the two people could have sex), which I knew meant that she wasn't ready to discuss those particular lyrics with me yet.

STEP 4: ASK THE RIGHT QUESTIONS

Initiating a meaningful conversation about relationships also starts with asking your child the right types of questions. Many parents try hard to find the right time or place, give consideration to their child's age and gender, and believe they know their child well, but still feel they are unsuccessful in bringing up the topic of relationships. They report resistance through anger, an "attitude," or just outright ignoring them.

Part of the reason why children get defensive or won't engage in these conversations is that you may not be *asking questions*—and, instead, are lecturing about what is right and wrong. Parents also like to talk about what they did when they were that age, leaving their child's own experiences out of the conversation. Even more off-putting, parents may not listen to their child's end of the conversation or acknowledge what their child is trying to contribute. Even when parents do ask questions, a child's irritated or disinterested response can often mean they aren't asking the *right kinds of* questions. If your child is resistant or defensive when you try to talk with them, try not to take it personally and instead think about how to ask the right kinds of questions.

How to ask the right kinds of questions

Asking the "right questions" can fall into four different categories. You might try one or all of these. Pay attention to your child and formulate your questions according to what approach will work best for them.

1. **Ask open-ended questions.** Closed-ended questions, such as "Are you dating anyone?" or "Do you like your new girlfriend?" require a one-word answer. Parents then feel they have to chase down information when they want to discuss important issues with their child. Instead, make a habit of asking open-ended questions, which require thought, such as:

- What was an interesting thing that happened to you today?

- What qualities are you attracted to in your new girlfriend?

- Which of your friends would you talk to if you needed help with something?

- What were some of the things your friends did over spring break?

2. **Ask specific questions.** Parents often bring up topics within the context of what is going on in their *own* lives— what the parent is reading, watching, or talking about with others. Instead, try to ask questions that focus on people or events important *to your child*. Even if it isn't your favorite topic of discussion, inquire about what movies, music, sports games, or friends they are interested in.

3. **Ask responsive questions.** You have your own agenda or message that you want to get across when you start a conversation, but be sure to listen to what your child is saying. Reflect before asking the next set of questions. You might be thinking so hard about what you will say next that you forget to hear what they are saying. The best questions are ones that focus on your child's questions, answers, or concerns. Children pay more attention to discussions regarding sex and relationships when parents are responsive—when they allow an authentic give-and-take conversation instead of a one-sided lecture. Parental responsiveness in discussions about sex and relationships also is associated with lower levels of sexual risk-taking by adolescents.

4. **Ask personal questions.** As your child becomes a young adult, the best questions are also ones that ask them

to think outside the box or that make them picture themselves in different scenarios. In my house, we often play the "personal question" game. Each family member thinks of an insightful question to ask everyone else, such as, "If you could travel anywhere in the world, where would you go and why?" "What are you most proud of doing in the last year?" or "What superpower do you wish you could have and why?" Questions that engage your child in interesting conversations take the form of asking how they would approach or react to challenging or funny situations. These types of questions stimulate your child's imagination, get them to think critically about relationships and how they interact with those around them, and give you insight into how they view the world and their place in it.

REVIEWING THE STEPS FOR STARTING IMPORTANT CONVERSATIONS

How well have you laid the groundwork for having important relationship discussions with your child? This is the first part toward positive and meaningful parent-child talks. You will want to make sure that your foundation is sound before embarking on the actual conversations, which we begin to explore in the next chapter. Are all systems go?

Recap

Let Go of Your Own Personal Emotional Baggage

- Try to identify and unpack any heavy emotional baggage that is weighing you down and that could sabotage what you share about relationships with your child.

- Find healthy outlets to release intense emotions associated with past relationships through physical or creative activities, spending time with friends and family, journaling about your experiences, or talking to a therapist or counselor if you can't get past your anger or frustration.

Pick the Right Time and Situation

- Consider the distractions that can get in the way of having a meaningful talk and understand when it is best to postpone starting a discussion.

- Set aside special time for one-on-one conversations outside your child's normal routines.

- Build in regular times when family members check in with each other to establish open communication between parent and child and let everyone know that what they say is valued.

Consider the Age, Gender, and Maturity of Your Child

- Determine what conversations are appropriate for your child in terms of their age, gender, maturity level, and kinds of relationships they are engaged in.

- Take cues from your child with regard to what they are ready to hear and when, depending upon the questions they ask, what they see and hear in shows and social settings, their level of interest, and what they experience through their own development.

- Start discussions about body parts and reproduction early— your child is exposed to more sexual terms and images than you may realize.

Ask the Right Questions

- When you meet with resistance or defensiveness, make sure that you are asking the right kinds of questions in your relationship conversations: open-ended, specific, and responsive questions, and those that address your child personally.

CHAPTER 3

Show Gratitude and Appreciation

When was the last time you thanked your partner, child, or other family members for being in your life? How often do you show the important people in your life that you value them? When we're busy and stressed, we often forget to thank the very people who are important to us.

If thanking your loved ones is something you only do once a year, or not at all, it is time you changed your ways. Why? *Because saying thanks and showing gratitude can greatly improve the health and happiness of a relationship!* When people feel appreciated in a relationship, they're happier in that relationship and more motivated to make the relationship better and stronger. In addition, by showing and teaching your child how to express gratitude in their relationships, you can have a significant effect on their overall emotional and physical well-being, the happiness in their love relationships, and the lifelong relationship that you have with your child. Simple expressions of affirmation are easy to model and implement.

One simple act of affirmation that I started when my son was in middle school was to text him after school every day. My texts would say something affectionate, like: "Thinking of you. I love you;" or "I am always so proud of you;" or "You are the best of the bestest!" To this day, I continue that tradition whenever I think he needs to hear a small affirmation from someone—and he is now 6 feet 5 inches tall and 24 years old. Small acts or phrases are as good as big ones, no matter your child's age.

How important is it to thank your loved ones? Consider this: In my long-term study of romantic couples, receiving affirmation or appreciation often from your partner, *particularly for men*, was the **#1 factor in predicting whether couples stayed together or not, over time.** For the happy couples, gratitude came in the form of words, gestures, or acts that showed the other partner that they were noticed, appreciated, and loved. Further, couples who expressed frequent gratitude to each other were the happiest in their relationships by a significant margin. In fact, 61% of the happy couples in my study said that their partners "often" made them feel good about the kind of person they are, compared to only 27% of the other couples.

Relationship Advice in Action

"[The one quality I would like in a relationship for my children is] to be in relationships with people who appreciate them for who they are and support them."
—*relationship survey response*

So far, you have learned that if you want your child to have happy, healthy love relationships you need to establish a trusting environment, help them reduce frustration and set realistic relationship expectations, and lay the groundwork for relationship discussions together. Once you know and understand how to put these steps into practice, you are ready for the next step in your journey. In this chapter, you'll discover what gratitude means and why it adds to self-worth and a positive self-image. I'll give you specific ways to express gratitude through words and actions, since science shows that there are clear emotional and physical health benefits to feeling affirmed by the important people in your life. I'll also discuss why affirmation is vital for your child's love relationships, and how you can model it. In addition, I'll address four conversations to have with your child about gratitude. Along the way, you'll learn two strategies to receive more affirmation from your loved ones, if you or your child is feeling underappreciated or ignored. I am confident that the information you learn in this chapter will be *extremely helpful* to your relationships and those of your child.

WHAT IS GRATITUDE AND WHY IS IT IMPORTANT?

Gratitude, or affirmation, consists of words, gestures, or acts that show others that they are noticed, appreciated, respected, loved, and desired. You can express gratitude in any number of ways: by giving a hug when someone feels down; sending a text in the middle of the day saying, "I'm thinking about you"; or voicing a compliment when a loved one puts on a new outfit or gets a new haircut. Expressions of gratitude are simple to give, and they say to others: "I see you, I notice you, and you matter!"

Business managers know that employees perform best when they receive frequent positive feedback. The same holds true for people in relationships. Research[8] finds that when you feel appreciated by loved ones, you're less likely to feel anxious and depressed (or feel like you don't matter), and you experience fewer headaches, a boosted immune system, and better heart health. In fact, the whole world seems better when you're noticed and appreciated.

Further, when another person in a relationship makes you feel important and well cared for, it is easy to reciprocate, and you feel happy to be in that relationship. Part of having a happy relationship is learning how to show the people you love appreciation for who they are and gratitude for what they add to your life.

SIMPLE TIP: Close Your Eyes and Imagine

Close your eyes for a minute. Think of the last time someone gave you a compliment or did something nice for you. This could be from a friend, love partner, child, relative, or even a stranger. What did they say or do? How did you feel after they expressed the compliment or did the nice thing for you? Remember how good this feels as you read this chapter and how important it is to model and talk to your child about this vital strategy for their happy, healthy love relationships.

Relationship Advice in Action

"[The number one key factor to a happy healthy relationship is] to make time to remember why you are together and make efforts and take time for each other."
—*relationship survey response*

When I observe happy couples in my study and therapy practice, they all share one common trait: The partners give each other affirmation on a regular basis. I also know that as a university professor, it is important that I notice each and every student, even when I have 50 or 100 students enrolled in my classes. I walk around every classroom, making sure I stop and say hello to as many students as I can. I have even adapted this process on Zoom, because I'm currently teaching online university courses, given the COVID-19 pandemic. I also take attendance from a student list every class period. Even though this takes time, the goal for me is to make sure every student knows: I see you, I notice you, and you matter to me.

MODELING AFFIRMATION WITH YOUR CHILD

The reason why gratitude is so important is that people have a psychological need to be needed. We all want to be noticed and feel that we matter to the important people around us. This recognition makes us human and, similar to our biological needs to eat, sleep, and drink, it is integral for human survival. Regardless of age, your child has a psychological need to feel loved, noticed, and valued by *you*. Studies show that all people in relationships have a basic need to feel valued and seen and the best part is that it takes very little to meet this essential need.

Now, I understand how you may think your child doesn't appreciate, or even recognize, all that you do for them. You are not alone in that feeling. I have had clients complain that they go to countless parent-teacher conferences, band concerts, graduations, award ceremonies, celebrations, and the like, to support their kids, and they help their children in many other ways, with little thanks. In fact, some parents are ignored or even snubbed by their children for showing up to support them. Still, it is important to recognize that, even if they don't outwardly look excited or directly tell you they appreciate your support and help, your presence and your love really do matter.

As a psychologist and a mother, I have observed that children, regardless of age, crave parental affirmation. Even when your child is an adult, they still need to be recognized and noticed by you. The best way to give affirmation is to convey you care through words and actions you tend to use every day, like greeting them when they come in the door, calling them to just say hi, and hugging or listening to them when they seem upset. Remember to focus on what is going right or is positive in your child's life, instead of only concentrating on or amplifying what is wrong. Here are some simple ways to share with your child how special they are to you:

- Send them a funny text message or photo in the middle of the day.

- Hug them for no reason.

- Say "I love you," or "Keep up the good work," when they appear stressed or tired.

- Watch their favorite TV show with them.

- Ask them if you can help them with something.

- Make them their favorite meal or dessert.

- Ask them to video chat, Zoom, or FaceTime with you.

- Tell them how much you enjoyed an outing together.

- Tell them know how proud you are of them for any accomplishment.

- Notice when they do something special for another person.

- Give them time and attention when they have something to share, and laugh together, sympathize, or give encouragement in response.

- Let them know when you learn from them.

- Give them a warm greeting when they come home or when you meet up.

- Compliment them for their special qualities.

- Text them often to say, "Thinking of you," or "You are amazing."

When my children were very young, I started writing special affirmations to them in their birthday cards. To this day, I continue to hand write special qualities that they each possess in these cards, like "Happy birthday! I want you to remember that you are kind, generous, smart, empathic, funny, and caring." The list of qualities grows each year. Although my children roll their eyes and laugh when they read the messages, I know they recognize and value the affirmations.

When you make your child feel special and important, they will not only feel better about themselves, but they will be more likely to respond with gratitude to you and others. It also gives your child the foundation and solid footing to discuss relationships with you, and to consider and put your advice into practice

How else can you share and model affirmation to your child? You can also show appreciation and gratitude in your acquaintance relationships, or those daily interactions with people you barely know, and model affirmation for your child at the same time. Recently, I observed the number of people I talked to in a single afternoon, which included my son's former baseball coach, two students, a client, a custodian at my office building, a coworker, and a woman at the gym. I had also emailed several people, most of whom I have never met in person. In fact, Americans spend more time with coworkers, clients, neighbors, and other acquaintances than with family and friends, according to recent studies.[9] While acquaintances will never replace your close relationships, research finds that positive connections with acquaintances provide distinct benefits to one's health.

Dr. Karen Fingerman, a family researcher, studies what she calls *non-intimate ties*, or acquaintance relationships. Her research finds that in American culture, most people report a few core ties and hundreds of peripheral or non-intimate ties. Close ties are essential for individuals' well-being, but peripheral ties may also be instrumental in allowing individuals to flourish. Her point is that we depend on these acquaintance relationships for many purposes. They reduce loneliness, help us problem-solve, provide fun, assist in everyday tasks as well as emergencies, and connect us to various religious, political, professional, and social groups. People with fewer of these ties are more likely to abuse alcohol and/or smoke too much.

The take-away? Your casual friends and acquaintances are the glue that holds your day-to-day life together. These relationships also deserve your attention and consideration. Show small acts of kindness to these acquaintances. Make an effort to connect with these people and get to know them a little more as individuals. And, when you do, your daily encounters will become richer and more fulfilling—both for you and for them. In addition, these behaviors and expressions of affirmation within your acquaintance relationships will also be observed and experienced by your child. By viewing your expressions of gratitude, your child (again) will learn how to treat and give gratitude to the people around them and in their love relationships.

What can you do to strengthen your connections with acquaintances and model appreciation of others to your child? Here are a few simple strategies that you can try when you meet people face-to-face or virtually on Zoom or FaceTime:

1. **Take a moment to connect.** Instead of rushing by your acquaintances—perhaps a co-worker you've passed dozens of times without talking to—slow down and talk to them. Do you know the person's first name? Do you know anything about them? Strike up a friendly conversation. Put time and energy into getting to know the people you interact with on a daily basis.

2. **Increase your eye contact.** Walking or talking to others with your eyes down or on your electronic device keeps you from seeing who's around you and prevents you from connecting with others. Instead, make eye contact, greet people, wish someone "good morning," or ask them how their day is going. A big smile from an acquaintance is extremely contagious. It will make both of you feel better.

3. **Open your mind.** When you don't know someone well, you may make assumptions about them based on superficial observations—their accent or their style of dress, for example. Take some time to get to know them a little better by striking up a conversation. The more interaction you initiate, the more understanding you become of acquaintances' perspectives. Make the most of these bonds. Besides, you never know who might be able to help you in the future or connect you to a valuable network.

4. **Don't scowl and growl.** When you're in a bad mood, you sometimes project your negativity onto strangers and acquaintances, figuring they don't really matter that much anyway. If you did this to a loved one or friend, they would confront you about it! If you're having a bad day, don't transfer that negativity to the acquaintances you run into or see. Instead, release your anger in constructive ways, such as through exercise, journaling, or art. Go outside and smell the flowers in your garden. Breathing fresh air is always a stress releaser. If outside is too chilly, walk around the mall at a good speed and people watch.

FOUR IMPORTANT CONVERSATIONS TO HAVE WITH YOUR CHILD

It's also important to sit down and talk to your child about expressing affirmation in their relationships—both romantic and non-romantic. The following four conversations cover topics about affirmation or gratitude for all children, regardless of age. Depending on the age of your child, and whether they are currently in a love relationship, you can have these conversations with them about:

1. A current love relationship

2. A current friendship

3. Their close relationships in general

As you share the multiple messages with your child, they will better understand that affirmation is expressed through *both* words and actions, they will identify how *they* want to receive affirmation from others, they will understand who needs it most—males or females—and they will learn what to do if they feel ignored or unappreciated in a relationship. These conversations will educate your child on the vital role that affirmation plays in *all* close relationships, particularly their love relationships. Look at each conversation and decide where it is best to begin.

Conversation #1: Simple Ways to Give Affirmation— All Relationships

One conversation to have with your child relates to **how they can express their gratitude, and explores specific examples.** Fulfilling another person's need for self-worth and reassurance through positive affirmation can be accomplished in two ways. The first is by *saying,* and the second is by *doing.*

AFFIRMATION WITH WORDS: WHAT TO SAY

There are countless ways *to tell* a love partner, family member, or friend that you care about them. "Thank you" may be the most crucial two words you can say to someone, and the two words your partner or loved one most wants to hear. But you can also thank your partner or other person indirectly with a heartfelt compliment: "You're a great person." "You're the *best* friend." "I'm so glad you're in my life." "You are so special to me." These simple statements will help the other person feel loved, cared for, noticed, and valued.

Verbal gratitude does not necessarily need to be delivered face-to-face. You can express it over the phone, by text, in an email, or in a card. Sometimes a surprise phone call or text in the middle of the day delivers more bang than a compliment when you get home. Mailing a heartfelt thank-you card to your partner, friend, or loved one can be a surprisingly simple way to make them feel appreciated and noticed.

Still, instead of lightly flinging words or phrases of affirmation around, you can give the sentiment more oomph if you say it like you mean it. To do this, you need to understand what you value and appreciate about your loved one. The first step in giving verbal affirmation is to take a few minutes and write down five particular qualities you are most thankful for in a friend, partner, or loved one. For example:

1. He lets you vent about your day.

2. She makes the foods you love most to eat.

3. She is excited to see you.

4. He makes you laugh.

5. She is an amazing listener.

I guarantee that this simple exercise will put a smile on your face.

Depending on your child's age, you can either do this list-making together or share with them how to do it themselves. When your child is younger, help them develop their list of what they appreciate most in their friends, teachers, grandparents, or other special people. Then, after they develop their list, they can read it aloud to the person, write it on a card or in a note, or get help from you about how to share their "five qualities" in verbal affirmations.

When my children were younger, we started this exercise and created a list of five things they were thankful for in their lives to read during our Thanksgiving dinners. If their list contained people or relationships, we would talk about why telling these people they were important or valued can help them to feel loved. Sometimes we would need to extend the list to include others at the table so that no one would feel left out. They came up with endearing attributes that family members and friends still remember, from "Grandma always tells me I'm her favorite grandchild," to "Uncle David tells the funniest jokes," to "Cousin Sarah lets me take do-overs when I mess up my serve in ping-pong." We still do this exercise, and my children are 27 and 24 years old. It is never too late and your child is never too old to start this tradition.

AFFIRMATION WITH ACTIONS: WHAT TO DO

The other way of showing affirmation or gratitude is through your actions. The key here is to try to see the world through the other person's eyes. What does a love partner or friend need? Engage your child in thinking about another's habits or particular challenges someone is facing. Is a grandmother stressed out from caring for an ill family member? Make a home-cooked meal together to take over. Is your partner going through a phase of low self-esteem after being skipped over for a promotion? Give them more hugs and affection. It's not hard to show another person regularly, through small endearments, that they matter to you, and that you're thankful that they are in your life. Point out opportunities for giving affirmation to and showing gratitude.

When children see the world through other people's experiences and challenges, not only are they better able to convey affirmation to someone else, but they also develop an essential trait for later adulthood. That trait is *empathy*, which is a significant milestone and developmental outcome. Psychologists maintain that early in childhood, children cannot differentiate well between the self and others. When they are able to adopt perspectives of other people and feel concern for or sensitivity to those other people, they have developed the desirable trait of empathy. (As a side note, a new study by the global nonprofit organization Catalyst finds that empathy is one of the most important leadership skills. Empathic leaders in the workplace have employees who are more innovative and engaged, especially in times of crisis.)

Relationship Advice in Action

"Empathy, I would think, is pretty key [to a happy, healthy relationship]. I feel like many of the other aspects of a healthy relationship would organically grow if empathy for one's partner can be established." —*relationship survey response*

Conversation #2: Who Needs Affirmation Most?— Love Relationship

Another conversation to have with your child relates to understanding gender differences regarding affirmation or gratitude. One of the most significant and unexpected findings from my long-term study on relationships centers on who needs this love and positive feedback the most (from love partners), men or women. What do you think? Given what you see and hear in the media, I'm sure that many of you think that women need these simple acts of kindness and attention from their romantic partners more than men. Well, from my research and clinical work, that assumption is *incorrect*!

For the couples in my study, receiving enough affirmation and gratitude was a critical factor in how happy both partners said they were in the relationship. However, affirmation *was far more important for men* than it was for women. Men who did not receive regular affirmation from their partners became distressed and unhappy in their relationships. Now, if we view affirmation as an indication of how loved you feel, it makes sense that it would be important to relationship happiness. But why does it play a more significant role in men's relationship happiness?

Let's look at the reasons why and then explore how it might relate to your child. When relationship psychologists study women and men, they observe that women, as a rule, get lots of this good stuff—positive feedback and affirmation from others—every day. They get frequent compliments, smiles, encouragement, and subtle rewards from family, friends, coworkers, and even strangers. For me, even when I go into my regular coffee shop on my way to work in the morning, the people behind the counter often notice and remark on my new haircut, outfit, or shoes. That affirmation often makes me smile and lightens up my morning. Women need less affirmation from their love partners because they get *more* of it from others.

On the other hand, men are starved for affirmation and appreciation from their romantic partners because they get *less* of it from others. At least in American culture, you don't regularly hear men telling their male friends or co-workers, "I love your new haircut," or "You mean the world to me," or "Where did you get that shirt?" I'll never forget what happened when my son, who at 16 years old had very long hair, decided to get a buzz cut. It was a big change, and I loved the new style! He looked so different when he went to school the next day. When he came home, I asked him what his friends and classmates (we're talking 2,500 students!) had to say about his new haircut. He responded, "Mom, guys just don't say those sorts of things to other guys, even if they want to!" (OMG: How smart was that comment? You'll notice that he said, "even if they want to!")

In general, men don't typically experience closeness and intimacy with people other than their love partners at the same level of intensity as women do. When relationship researchers talk about intimacy, we don't mean sexual intimacy. Rather, intimacy is a feeling of intense connection or a close bond. And men simply don't get as much of this essential attention from their outside relationships because there are differences in how men and women "do" their same-sex friendships or promote closeness in their relationships with others. Some of this is due to innate differences between men and women, but in general, men and women manage their friendships differently because of variations in what we teach children to want out of their friendships. And this difference *starts very early in life*.

In general, studies[10] show that young boys engage in rough-and-tumble play with friends (wrestling, football, or other physical games) and spend more time in larger friendship groups. In contrast, young girls typically spend more one-on-one time with friends and their play is less physical and tends more toward personal interaction. These types of play and the close, intimate nature of the friendships girls form allow them to cooperate rather than compete. Girls also give affirmation to their playmates more frequently and more comfortably, which creates a sense of closeness. Boys, on the other hand, don't have the same approach in their friendships to give and receive affirmation and gratitude. Their style of play is more physical, more competitive, and less emotional.

In this second conversation with your child about why affirmation from love partners *is more vital to men than women,* the following key messages are useful to help them better understand the gender differences and the importance of expressing gratitude (regardless of gender) within their love relationships. You can help to change gender norms by talking to your child—whether boy or girl—about the importance of promoting connection and bonding in *all* of their relationships, including their same-sex friendships, and the value of expressing appreciation in those friendships and love relationships. If we teach our children the merit of expressing gratitude in all of their relationships, they will reap the many rewards.

THREE KEY MESSAGES TO EXPRESSING GRATITUDE, REGARDLESS OF GENDER

Three messages to discuss with your child, regardless of gender, about conveying affirmation and gratitude to friends can help them perceive—and potentially overcome—gender differences, realize why it is important in relationships, and consider how to express gratitude to their friends.

1. **Men and women are often different in their friendship experiences.** These differences are seen in what information is shared and what opportunities arise to support and share with one another. In general, women are taught and rewarded for giving emotional support to others and emotional sharing; men are neither taught nor rewarded for those same expressions. Beverly Fehr, a relationship researcher, finds that women share more personal information, provide more emotional support, and express more feelings of affection to their friends than men do.[11]

How to initiate the discussion: Have your child think about one of their same-sex friendships. Ask what kinds of activities they like doing with that friend. Describe how girls/women tend to spend more of their same-sex friendship time simply talking together (in person, texting, or on the phone). Boys/men, on the other hand, spend more of their time doing things together (including playing sports, watching TV, playing video games). Does that stereotype fit with their friendships? Could they do both types of activities in that friendship? Would that change their friendship? How do they think their friend would respond?

2. **Regardless of gender, expressions of affirmation and gratitude are essential in friendships and lead to greater happiness for each friend.** Your child likes it when a friend says or does something that shows they matter or are special.

   How to initiate the discussion: Have your child imagine that they're seeing a friend for the first time in many months. When they get together with the friend, the friend gives them a compliment ("You look amazing!" "I've missed you," or "It hasn't been the same without you"). Ask them how they would feel. What would they think about the friend? Are they more likely to connect and feel close to that friend? What simple expressions of gratitude or appreciation have made them feel special?

3. **It is easy to say or do something small to express appreciation in friendships.**

   How to initiate the discussion: Ask your child whether, if they really admired one of their friends, they would share that sentiment with their friend. Do they feel comfortable letting their friend know they admire them? Would that expression occur in private or public? Through a text or in person? How do they think that friend would respond? Would that change their friendship? What are some simple ways to tell that friend about how they feel? Is making an effort to spend time with a friend or including a friend in your games or activities enough to make them feel affirmed, or would sharing words of gratitude, such as "Thanks for being a good friend," or "I'm so in awe of what you do" seem more appropriate? When your child shows or tells their friends their gratitude, ask them to share their friends' reactions, how they felt expressing their gratitude, whether they'd change anything the next time, and if the friendship became stronger over time as a result.

MEASURE YOUR CHILD'S FEELINGS OF AFFIRMATION

Next, in the conversation with your child about why affirmation from love partners *is more vital to men than women,* ask about whether they feel affirmed in their current relationships. Have them take the affirmation quiz below, and then score their results with them. A good time to have them assess whether they feel appreciated in the friendship with their best friend, or in the relationship with their current love partner might be after a misunderstanding or disagreement. If they are currently in a love relationship that you aren't enamored with, this might be a wonderful opportunity for you to suggest they think about their romantic partner without sharing your negative opinion with them (I'll expand on this issue further in Chapter 8).

After they take the quiz and you score their results, discuss what their score means and ask them if they agree with the interpretation of their score. If your child wants to do this quiz on their own, that is fine too. You can ask them a few days later, "How are you feeling about the affirmation quiz results you took a few days ago?"

Asking about their impressions of the quiz and/or results, rather than just asking them for the results, increases the likelihood of your child opening up to you. And be sure to reassure them that if they don't feel affirmed in the friendship or love relationship, *there are ways to change or reverse that* (I'll cover this in Conversation #4).

QUIZ: How Affirmed Do You Feel by Your Love Partner/Best Friend?

Think about the connection with your love partner or best friend. How affirmed do you feel in that relationship? Rate each statement on a scale of 1 to 4, where: 1 = Never, 2 = Rarely, 3 = Sometimes, and 4 = Often.

1. In the past month, how often did you feel that your love partner/friend made you feel good about having your own ideas and ways of doing things?

   1 = Never
   2 = Rarely
   3 = Sometimes
   4 = Often

2. In the past month, how often did you feel your love partner/friend made you feel good about the kind of person you are?

   1 = Never
   2 = Rarely
   3 = Sometimes
   4 = Often

(continued)

3. In the past month, how often did you feel your love partner/friend was thoughtful and considerate toward you (listened to you, addressed your concerns, was helpful or supportive)?

1 = Never
2 = Rarely
3 = Sometimes
4 = Often

4. In the past month, how often did you feel your love partner/friend thanked you for something you did or said?

1 = Never
2 = Rarely
3 = Sometimes
4 = Often

Scoring: Add up the points from your responses

4–6 points   Your love partner/friend may care about you, but they aren't letting you know through words and actions that you matter. You likely feel ignored or taken for granted in this relationship.

7–9 points   Your love partner/friend notices you and gives you some attention, but you are likely not getting the affirmation you desire. Why is this important? Because lacking affirmation can lead to feeling neglected and dissatisfied in your relationship. The good news is that it's easy to reverse.

10–13 points   Your love partner/friend gives you affirmation occasionally. But you likely are still not completely satisfied and you would like to be more appreciated and valued. How can you ratchet up the affirmation you would like?

14–16 points   Your love partner/friend is making you feel wonderful about yourself and giving you affirmation regularly. How do you continue this pattern in your relationship? Are you *reciprocating* that affirmation?

Conversation #3: How to Identify What You Want to Receive—Love Relationship

My research study also shows that men and women often have different preferences for *how* they wish to receive affirmation.

In general, males are more likely to show than to tell affirmation. That is, they gravitate more to actions than to words, and they also respond more to actions than words. Thus, if someone is giving them a compliment, they may not hear the affirming words as much as if they see actions that represent appreciation. For example, you may say "I love you" to your son, but he may not hear it as affirmation unless you also accompany it with a hug or a kiss. In contrast, females tend to be more verbal, so if someone is showing gratitude, a woman or girl might not "get it" if the other person doesn't also say the words "thank you," "I appreciate you," or "I'm so grateful." For instance, you may make your daughter her favorite dessert, but she may not see it as gratitude or appreciation unless you accompany it with words of affirmation.

In addition to, or despite, these generalized gender differences, each person has an individual preference for how they like to receive affirmation or gratitude. Some people prefer words; others would like actions. Once your child understands their own personal style or preference, it will open their eyes and they'll be able to state their preferences to their love partner and friends. They'll be able to say, "I hear your words, but do your actions show me the same thing?" Or, "I would love for you to *show* me affirmation, rather than tell me with words." I'll share some strategies of how to communicate these preferences in Conversation #4 (see page 99).

It is important that your child pays attention to the two styles of receiving affirmation and understand whether they prefer to receive action-oriented, word-oriented, or both styles of affirmation. Learning how to get the affirmation you need from a love partner or friend will significantly predict the happiness and health of those relationships. We will discuss how to change the way you speak to get what you need and want in Chapter 4.

The following quiz will help your child assess their preferences for receiving affirmation. Have your child answer the statements below in terms of their connection with a current love partner or a best friend. If they are currently in a love relationship, encourage them to think of that relationship.

Then, score their answers together. Discuss what their score means and ask them if they agree with the interpretation of their score. If your child prefers to do the quiz on their own, that is fine. Come back after a few days and ask them for their impressions of the quiz and/or results.

QUIZ: Preference for Receiving Affirmation from a Love Partner/Best Friend

How do you want your love partner or friend to give you affirmation? What is your preferred way to feel appreciated?

1. When you have had a difficult day (at home, school, or work), which of the following do you typically prefer from your love partner/friend?

    1 = Saying something to make you feel better (e.g., "I love you," "I'm sorry you had a bad day," or "I'm here for you always")

    2 = Doing something to make you feel better (e.g., giving you a hug, holding you, or making your favorite meal)

    3 = Both saying *and* doing something to make you feel better

2. When you and your love partner/friend meet, which of the following do you typically prefer from your love partner/friend?

    1 = Saying something (e.g., "Great to see you," "Hey you!" or "I've missed you")

    2 = Doing something (e.g., a playful hug or a kiss)

    3 = Both physical contact *and* words of greeting

3. When you and your love partner/friend celebrate a special event (birthday, holiday, end of school year), which of the following do you typically prefer from your love partner/friend?

    1 = Saying something to make you feel special (e.g., sending you a text or Instagram message, writing something in a card, calling you, telling you they want to get together)

(continued)

> 2 = Doing something to make you feel special (e.g., buying you a special gift, taking you out for a meal or drink, getting together to spend time)
>
> 3 = Doing something together and *also* expressing their gratitude in words
>
> 4. Of the many ways that your love partner/friend can express their appreciation and gratitude to you, which of the following do you typically prefer from your love partner/friend?
>
> 1 = Saying something (e.g., giving compliments, texting or messaging often, finding different ways to say "You're a great friend")
>
> 2 = Doing something (e.g., hugging, spending time together, buying gifts, doing things you want to do, taking you out for a special treat)
>
> 3 = Saying something, together with a special gesture

Scoring: All or majority 1's: **You prefer to receive affirmation through words.** You tend to bask in the warm glow of appreciative words from your partner/friends, and actions may fall short of what you consider to be a true expression of gratitude. Be aware that others may be good at giving affirmation through actions, rather than words, so you may need to convey your preference to them.

All or majority 2's: **You prefer to receive affirmation through actions.** To you, actions speak more loudly than words, and you prefer for your partner/friends to show gratitude and appreciation through acts. Be aware that others may be good at expressing affirmation through words, rather than gestures, so you may need to convey your preference to them.

All or majority 3's: **You prefer to receive affirmation through** *both* **words and actions.** To you, an action with no words to describe its meaning holds less impact, and similarly, words without an accompanying action fall short in conveying their true meaning. Be aware that your partner/friends may not perceive that their words or actions alone aren't your preferred way to receive affirmation. You may need to convey this to them.

AT A GLANCE

Some people prefer neither words nor actions from their love partners. In general, they fear relationships and emotional expressions, or they don't want the attention on them. There are several reasons or traits (e.g., depression, autism spectrum disorders) for this that are beyond the scope of this book. Do not be alarmed; there are resources out there to get additional assistance and information. You can reach out to a teacher, coach, social worker, or therapist if your child says "none" to all of the questions in the quiz.

Conversation #4: How to Get More Affirmation from Others—All Relationships

Relationships with romantic partners, family members, and friends are not always equal when it comes to the giving and receiving of attention, affection, and affirmation. In fact, it is quite common to be in a relationship where you don't receive the same amount of gratitude as you give to someone else. This inequality, in the short-term, can be tolerated and not affect the relationship. But, if the imbalance continues over time, it can lead to emotional distress in one or both people in the relationship. Two types of imbalances can occur when it comes to affirmation: The first is if you *give more* affirmation than you receive in return. In the second, you *receive more* affirmation than you give. In the first instance, the inequity can cause you to feel anger, frustration, and disappointment. In the second instance, you may experience guilt, concern, and sadness knowing that the other person feels angry and frustrated.

In either situation, what can people do if they want to give or receive more affirmation in a close relationship? What can your child do if they discovered earlier in the chapter that they're feeling ignored or underappreciated in a relationship? From my research, and in my clinical and personal experience, I can say that **change is possible**. And you or your child can change the inequity in your relationships in one of two ways.

STRATEGY 1: EMPLOY THE LAW OF RECIPROCITY—GIVE MORE TO GET MORE

This first strategy is best for the child who is feeling underappreciated and doesn't want to rock the boat too much in a relationship. This method is also helpful for those who are shy or reserved, more hesitant about directly asking someone for more attention, or doubtful whether saying something will matter much. In this strategy, you give affirmation to get more back. In other words, display one gesture *and* say one expression of affirmation to a love partner or friend. The idea is that expressing affirmation to the other person and expressing it in both ways will lead the other person to reciprocate with an affirmation in return. Your child can select any of the simple expressions that we discussed previously in this chapter (see page 84) to express gratitude.

Over a few weeks, this strategy will nudge the other person toward new behavior, and soon the other person will affirm or appreciate them more often. In psychology, we call this principle the "law of reciprocity." We find that when one person in a close relationship gives affirmation each day, both verbally and behaviorally, for at least 21 days, *in most instances* it is human nature to return the appreciation in kind. Some people will respond to the behaviors and others will respond to the verbal affirmation—and some will respond to the two combined. As long as the gratitude or affirmation is obvious and consciously recognized by the partner, the reciprocity principle is likely to hold true.

STRATEGY 2: IDENTIFY HOW YOU WANT TO RECEIVE AFFIRMATION AND SHARE YOUR NEEDS

The second strategy is appropriate for your child who has a good sense of their needs when it comes to affirmation or gratitude in relationships. In this option, it is a good idea to have taken the quiz presented on page 97 and to have identified what type of affirmation is preferred—words or actions, or both combined.

Once your child has a good sense of their need for affirmation and the kind of affirmation desired, encourage them to talk with their love partner or friend about what type of affirmation they want or need. It is important that the discussion focus on what type of affirmation *they* want, rather than on what the other person isn't doing in the relationship.

The best way to initiate one of these conversations with a love partner or friend is to **first start with a positive statement**. For example: "I like our friendship," "I value you as my partner" or "Thank you for your support."

Then, ask the love partner or friend **if they are getting the attention or appreciation they deserve or need (from you).** In this second part of the discussion, your child is essentially asking if there is anything else they can do to make sure the love partner or friend knows that they are very special. Possible ways of saying this are, "Do you know how much I value/appreciate you in my life?" or "I want to make sure that I tell you that often enough."

The last part of the process is to **share how they would like to receive more frequent appreciation in the relationship, along with how that might look**. They can tell the other person, "I would love for you to also show me how special this friendship is to you," or "I'm feeling like I don't matter; can you tell me if this relationship is important to you?"

By using this three-step strategy, the hope is that after you have affirmed your partner/friend, and asked them if they feel appreciated, they will react less defensively and will more likely hear what you have to say when you tell them how you would like to receive more affirmation. I will continue to discuss how to help your child communicate better about their needs and wants in their relationships in Chapter 4.

REVIEWING THE IMPORTANCE OF SHOWING GRATITUDE AND APPRECIATION

When shared often, the **words, gestures, or acts** that show friends or loved ones they are **appreciated, respected, and loved** increase satisfaction and lead to more healthy relationships. It is important to teach your child **how to express gratitude and appreciation**, as well as how to identify and share their **own preferences for receiving affirmation** from love partners, friends, and loved ones.

Recap

People have a psychological need to feel valued in their relationships.

- Affirmation or gratitude are words or acts that show others they are noticed, appreciated, and valued.

- By giving your child affirmation, they will not only be healthier physically and psychologically, but they'll also feel better about themselves and be more likely to reciprocate with gratitude to you and others. It will also lead to happier and healthier love relationships.

- Look for moments when you can share with your child, through words or gestures, how special they are.

- Teach your child how to express affirmation to family, friends, and in their love relationships.

Expressions of gratitude are simple to give, and they express to others: "I see you, I notice you, and you matter!"

- In my research, particularly for men, receiving frequent affirmation from their love partner was the *number one factor* in predicting whether couples stayed together over time.

- When you receive affirmation, you're happier, you're more motivated to work on your relationship, and you feel better physically and psychologically.

- Relationships where people express frequent gratitude to each other are the happiest by a significant margin.

Model for your child how to share affirmation with others.

- Express your gratitude for them.

- Make an effort to connect with and show small acts of kindness to acquaintances, or non-intimate others. These encounters will be more fulfilling for you, too.

Talk to your child about how to express affirmation in their relationships, and why it is important.

- They can convey appreciation by *saying* it through words or *showing* it through actions; people have their own preference for receiving expressions of affirmation.

- Generally, males receive far less affirmation and gratitude than females in their day-to-day lives and need more from their love partners.

- Boys and girls are socialized to give and receive affirmation and gratitude differently, and it's important to address these differences.

- If your child doesn't receive enough affirmation from their love partner or best friend, they can either share their need to be shown more appreciation or, by offering more displays of gratitude themselves, they can make the other person more likely to reciprocate.

CHAPTER 4

Change the Way You Speak

I've got some good news and some bad news when it comes to communication. The bad news: if kids don't learn to communicate in their love relationships, they will always have unhappy relationships. Miscommunication leads to frustration, conflict, and relationship dissatisfaction. The good news: *you* can do something about it. It's up to you to model effective communication and talk to your child about communication in relationships. And when I say communication, I don't just mean with words.

When my children were young teens and we were delayed somewhere, we passed the time by observing strangers' conversations. I called it "The Relationship Guessing Game." My son and daughter would watch the people around them and try to guess the kind of relationship between them (i.e., friend, parent-child, spousal, dating, sibling, co-worker). We took our clues from how loudly people talked, their tone of voice, their amount of eye contact, how closely they stood or sat together, and whether they touched each other. My kids and I loved this game! The best part was describing the reasoning behind the conclusions we drew. We never knew whether our guesses were right or wrong, but it didn't matter. It was my made-up game to not only pass the time, but to teach them about the role tone of voice, facial expression, and body language play in communication between people and how it differs according to the type of relationship.

Communication is the means by which people convey information to others about their feelings, ideas, and intentions. The specific words and behaviors used to convey or transmit the information make a *huge* difference in how others understand you. Both verbal and nonverbal communication have tremendous influence over the health and well-being of all interpersonal relationships. The process of good communication—when information is effectively conveyed from one person to another—is critical to the satisfaction and success of that relationship. In fact, studies show that romantic partners, friends, and family members who communicate poorly with each other are very dissatisfied with and unhappy in their relationships. If you want your child to have happy and satisfying relationships, they *must* learn how to communicate effectively, both verbally and nonverbally. Good communication (saying what you mean, hearing what others want you to hear, and having your nonverbal gestures mean what you want them to) is essential and ***the key to a happy love relationship***.

Communication might seem like it should be simple between people within a love relationship, but it is actually very complex. It is not easy to say what you mean, and it is extremely difficult to listen to (and hear!) what others are saying or intending to share. More often than most realize, people in relationships face what is commonly known as "miscommunication," when the message one person sends is not the same message that the other person hears or understands. Miscommunication in relationships can be frustrating for both members, because we all want to be heard and understood.

Here is a classic example to illustrate miscommunication and how easily it can happen. A young adult is sitting on the couch watching television with their parent. At the end of the program, the child says to the parent, "Let's go out for dinner tonight." These words can be interpreted in two ways by the parent. Does the child mean, "Let's get out of the house, just the two of us, and go somewhere special," which is a positive comment? Or "I am tired of your cooking, I want something else to eat," which has a negative connotation?

The parent can hear either meaning in the child's statement, and that doesn't even account for the tone of voice (energetic and inquiring or mumbling and apathetic), facial expression (smiling or bored), or body language (looking directly at the parent or facing forward with arms crossed). These nonverbal expressions can add to or confuse the message received. When the child intended to convey the first message, "Let's go out somewhere special, just the two of us," but the parent interpreted it to mean the latter, "I'm tired of your cooking," miscommunication has happened!

HELPING YOUR KID LEARN HOW TO COMMUNICATE: SHOWING AND TELLING

You've learned that to help your child have happy, healthy relationships you need to practice relationships as a priority, initiate important relationship conversations, and show gratitude. Next, it's time to help your child learn how to communicate well. This chapter is divided into two sections. The first part discusses different types of verbal and nonverbal communication, and three reasons why miscommunication typically occurs in relationships. In the second part of the chapter, you'll learn strategies to effectively communicate in relationships. You'll discover how to share this vitally important information with your child so they can more easily convey their feelings and intentions, and interpret those of others, when they communicate. You'll also need to model and participate in these good communication techniques. The goal is to help your child gain the necessary skills to effectively communicate in all of their relationships. And the outcome is that they'll be happier and more satisfied in their love relationships, and at the same time, you'll be paving the road to a better lifelong relationship with them.

Relationship Advice in Action

"Communication—it builds intimacy, which builds on trust. It's the foundation." —*relationship survey response*

I show a video in all of my classes, speaking engagements, and relationship workshops that cleverly illustrates how the way in which we craft our message makes a tremendous difference. The video, "The Power of Words,"[12] starts with a blind man on the street sitting next to a cardboard sign and a can for donations. His sign reads: "I'm blind, please help." A few passersby put coins in the can, but not many. A woman walks by, stops, and turns back. She flips the cardboard over and writes a new message with a black marker she fishes out of her pocket, and then walks on. Suddenly, every person walking by is giving the man change.

The woman returns later in the day, and the man says, "What did you do to my sign?" She answers, "I wrote the same, but in different words." We then see how she revised his sign to read: "It's a beautiful day and I can't see it!" The video illustrates perfectly the multiple ways you have of communicating your message to another person. As the creator of the video, Andrea Gardner, states, "Change your words, change your world."

In this chapter, you'll discover how to share this vital message with your child: ***By changing the way you communicate, you can experience healthier love relationships!***

TWO TYPES OF COMMUNICATION

People convey information through both verbal and nonverbal communication. For example, let's say Jose comes home unexpectedly. His partner Jeremy greets Jose with the verbal message, "Hi, honey. You're home early! How was your day?" At the same time, however, Jeremy doesn't move from his computer, he doesn't smile or go to hug him, and he gets right back to the email icon on his screen. His words may say he's happy to see his partner, but his body language and behaviors are sending another message. They are saying: "I'm really busy right now. Why are you here?" We will discuss a bit later how it's important to pay attention to both the verbal and the unspoken messages you receive from others to understand the full meaning of what is being communicated. Your body language can reveal wonders to the other person about what you really feel or think.

Verbal communication

Language is the primary way that people communicate with one another. In this chapter we are mainly interested in the verbal communication that occurs between two people in close relationships. Language allows us to express to others how we feel and what we think. It also provides us with a means to convey our experiences to others who may not directly share that experience. The specific words we speak or write are vital to how and whether another person understands and receives the message we wanted to transmit. As a relationship scientist, I study how spoken language is used in interactions within relationships. This involves observing how verbal communication can have consequences for the health and well-being of those in a relationship.

In every language, multiple words can express the same concept. For example, "love," "admire," "respect," "appreciate," "desire," "adore," and "revere" convey similar meanings. Yet, the specific word you select when talking to someone can convey particular information and feelings toward that other person. You need to be deliberate about the words you choose when you're speaking, because each word, as the list above shows, actually imparts a particular feeling or level of intensity.

For example, if two teens are dating for several months and the guy says to his girlfriend, "I admire you," she may infer that he has decided to just be her friend. She may get angry or withdraw from him because she is hurt by what she thought his words convey. He may have intended to say, "I love you" or "I'm in love with you," but instead used a word that his girlfriend interpreted to more closely describe friendship than love. This miscommunication could be damaging to the relationship. Later on in this chapter, you'll learn how to make sure verbal communication isn't misunderstood.

In this chapter, I focus on verbal communication that involves face-to-face conversations. Some of the information can also be applied to conversations over the telephone. Computer-mediated communication (CMC) or communicating with others from a distance via a computer or other digital device has become very common, where specific words are written in an email, text, or other social media message, but all body language and paralanguage (vocal cues) are removed. In other words, there are no additional auditory or visual clues to help others understand the context of the written message. This can make it difficult to fully comprehend the information being shared. Because young adults these days use CMC regularly, they are less apt to learn how to communicate effectively or how to merge nonverbal and verbal communication. That is why it is even more vital to talk and model effective communication strategies with your child. We will further discuss how computer-mediated communication and other forms of communication aided by technology (e.g., online dating sites and apps) can affect relationships in Chapter 7.

SIMPLE TIPS: Five Ways to Communicate with Bosses, Teachers, and Other Higher-ups

The rest of the world may consider Americans to be especially casual in our social interactions. But that doesn't mean we're without certain protocols when it comes to showing due respect for those above us in age or position. Talk to your child about communicating appropriately with adults who are authority figures in their lives, including professors, friends' parents, bosses, neighbors, and coaches by sharing the below tips. Remember that the way you talk to others both online and off teaches your child to do the same.

- When being introduced, look the person in the eye, shake hands firmly, and say, "It's nice to meet you."

- Use the person's sir name and the appropriate courtesy title (Mrs., Ms., Mr., Dr., Professor) unless they ask you to refer to them in another way.

- Greet them by name when you see them in passing.

- If you email them a message, use a more formal salutation than "Hi" (preferably "Dear" before the name, and never "Hey"). Use full sentences and words, rather than abbreviations and slang words (e.g., "u" for you or "K" for okay).

- Don't use swear words or crass expressions.

Nonverbal communication

Nonverbal communication is the manner by which we transmit information to another person *without* words or language. Although your child may not be as consciously aware of the power and influence of nonverbal communication, it is just as critical—*if not more*—as verbal communication to healthy love relationships. In fact, when there is a discrepancy between what is said and the nonverbal behavior displayed, the truth is exhibited through the nonverbal communication. That's because our behaviors are less under our control than our words, are more likely to "appear" when we are nervous or lying, and are harder to change.

Honesty between two people builds trust in a relationship. When one person has secrets or withholds information from the other person, it violates the expectations of a trusting relationship. Studies show that people tell at least one lie per week.[13] The lies may be small and harmless, or they may be big and serious. Even the harmless ones can destroy a relationship if they're frequent enough. No one "sign" is associated with telling a lie, but patterns in how a person behaves offer clues. If you observe repetition in the behaviors below, it may be a sign that a partner or friend is lying to you.

1. **Evasiveness**

   A person may become less forthcoming when you ask them questions and it will begin to feel like pulling teeth to have a conversation. When asked direct questions, your partner or friend may avoid answering the questions directly or say "I don't know" a lot. If this isn't how the person typically behaves, then it can be a signal that something is up.

2. **Speech Patterns**

   When people are lying, they often speak hesitantly, in a higher pitch, and they make more grammatical errors and slips of the tongue than when they tell the truth. There are discrepancies or mismatches between their tone of voice and their facial expressions. They may even cover their mouth while talking. It is as if they're subconsciously repressing the untruths they're saying. It may be as blatant as completely concealing the mouth, or as subtle as a single finger placed in front of the lips.

3. **Body Talk**

Often, when someone is lying, the mouth and the body are out of sync. The words sound convincing, but everything else about the body sends a different message. If your partner or friend can't look you in the eye, this may mean that they have something to hide. People who lie tend to blink more often out of nervousness that they'll be caught in their lie.

A great deal of research has focused on nonverbal communication and its connection to happiness in love relationships. Studies show that couples who can accurately send and receive nonverbal communication are happier in their relationships. Why? It may be the case that partners' good nonverbal skills lead to less confusion and conflict, which equals more happiness in relationships. It is just as likely that happier couples work harder at communicating nonverbally. That's why it's important to talk to your child about nonverbal communication—they might not interpret it as easily as you do.

Findings[14] also demonstrate that women are better at sending and reading nonverbal messages than men. Women do better at nonverbal communication because, in general, they have more learned skills (e.g., women spend more time watching others' eyes than men do; women are better able to read facial expressions than men) and they have greater motivation to accurately communicate nonverbally. The good news, however, is that both men and women can improve the accuracy with which they receive and send nonverbal communication. Later on in this chapter, you'll learn how to make sure nonverbal communication is not misunderstood.

COMPONENTS OF NONVERBAL COMMUNICATION

Nonverbal communication contains many different components. First, you can convey information to another person through *paralanguage*, which is aspects of speech other than words—such as the rhythm, pitch, volume, and rate of your voice. For example, when you're speaking to your child, you may raise your voice to accentuate what you're saying or to make sure they're paying attention. Your child becomes aware that you need them to listen more from the cue of your raised voice than from the information imparted in your words.

When my children were young and I saw one of them reaching for a hot pan or opening the car door before I'd stopped completely, I would modulate my voice by speaking slowly or raising my voice (not yelling, but speaking more loudly than usual) to communicate that I needed their attention. Afterwards, I would tell them why I altered my voice—why it was louder or my speech was slower—and ask how it affected them. My goal was to teach them how paralanguage ("tone of voice") transmits information that is important. By paying attention to another's tone of voice, you can be sure to hear the information someone is trying to get across.

Body language is another type of nonverbal communication and refers to all the movements of the body, including gesturing with the hands, crossing the arms in front of the body, straightening or curling posture, and leaning in or away with the body, to communicate information. I can tell how my son is feeling on any particular day (and my students, too), by observing his posture as he enters a room. My son is tall, and when he feels confident and happy, he walks with his head up, his shoulders back, and an alert expression in his eyes. On days when he feels down, he slouches with his arms crossed in front of his body, and he avoids eye contact.

When I give dating advice to singles, I discuss how body language, when you walk into a room full of people or meet another person, is one of the most critical pieces of information you project about yourself without even saying a word. This is important advice for first dates (and job interviews). Sitting with a date at a table and leaning away from the person with your arms crossed in front of you conveys that you're not available, not relaxed in the situation, and not interested. When you stand and sit tall, lean slightly forward as you talk and listen to your date, and keep your arms at your sides with your hands relaxed, you convey interest and availability. I will discuss more dating advice that you can share with your child in Chapter 7, but studies[15] show that these body gestures convey information to others, particularly when we are referring to love relationships.

Facial expressions can also convey information to others. Your mood and emotions are often clearly shown on your face. An especially interesting research finding[16] about nonverbal communication is that of all the components, facial expressions are the most universal. In other words, our basic facial expressions impart the same general emotions across all cultures. Research shows that even babies can recognize the meanings behind facial expressions, which illustrates how early in life this component of communication is learned. The universal meanings of our facial expressions make them very informative.

You can share an activity with your child to help them understand how their facial expressions often display their mood or emotions. In my family, we did this with my son and daughter by playing a form of charades. We took a piece of paper, tore it into several pieces, and wrote an emotion on each slip of paper (sadness, fear, surprise, anxiety, joy). My children took turns picking them out of a hat, and each of us made expressions that we thought displayed the emotion. This game is a simple and fun way to help your child interpret how different facial expressions convey important unspoken information. I even use this exercise with my college students in the classroom to drive the point home to them.

Interpersonal spacing or *proxemics* is another nonverbal communication tool that is extremely important in relationships. People convey information about the type of relationship they want or have with someone by the amount of physical space they place between themselves and another person. The closer the proximity to one another, the more intimate the relationship. Friends and romantic partners interact within shorter proximities, while the amount of distance increases among acquaintances and work/school relationships. These distances, however, vary greatly by culture and gender in society. For example, women interact with one another at closer distances then men do in Western cultures. When strangers violate our expectations of what we think is appropriate in terms of personal space and come too close to us, we move away or experience discomfort. The COVID-19 pandemic has definitely made us more acutely aware of the spacing between people.

For example, I teach a large lecture course with about 150 students, and many of the students come talk with me after class and ask questions, which I always enjoy because it shows me that students are connecting with the material. A few years ago, one international student stayed after class to talk with me, but entered into my personal space as we spoke, standing about a foot away from me. This made me feel uneasy and I found myself backing up. To me, such proximity is appropriate only for those with whom I have an intimate relationship, and I wasn't comfortable at that range in our professor-student relationship. Research findings[17] back me up on this: Americans only interact at that distance with their romantic partners. Eventually, I sat down with him and shared how interpersonal space varies within relationships and, in America, students and professors allowed more space between each other. This was a learning experience for us both.

Here are two simple ways to help your child recognize nonverbal communication. You might initiate the below exercises or games, introducing the activity as something fun and laughter-producing to do together, rather than as something that will teach them about nonverbal communication. For example, you might say, "Hey, I read this interesting book today that shared a fun activity that we can do together. The book says the activity is sure to make us all laugh. Want to try it with me, as long as we have some extra time at dinner tonight?"

1. **Imitation game**

   Sitting around a table, ask each person to take a turn imitating the person to their right. Try to capture the person's voice (paralanguage), facial expressions, and body language. You can decide to imitate the person in a particular context (when they wake up in the morning, while playing a sport, or talking in front of a group of people), or just in general. The role-playing can last a few seconds or a few minutes. After everyone has a turn, switch directions so that you now impersonate the person to the left (the one you imitated before now gets to imitate you). Playing this game always leads to lots of laughter, but also indirectly teaches your child to watch for nonverbal communication cues, to understand what these signals mean, and to see how easily nonverbal gestures or expressions can be misunderstood.

   Although this game is most appropriate for high schoolers (ages 16–17), my family continued to enjoy it until my children were in their mid-20s! Also, watching my children mimic me in speech and facial expressions was hilarious, and actually gave me some feedback on my own verbal and nonverbal behaviors. (I never knew they thought my eyes popped open so much when I smiled!) I also loved imitating my daughter when she was 16 or 17 years old. I pretended I was going into her room at 6 in the morning on school days. I would knock on the door and say in a soft and calming voice, "Good morning, sweetie. I love you. Are you up?" Then I'd imitate my daughter frowning and clenching her teeth. I'd growl with a high-pitched loud voice and say, "Leave me alone!" The entire family, including my daughter, would all cry with laughter. We could then discuss how we all could tell what kind of a mood she was in. (My daughter never was a morning person.) The nonverbal paralanguage and facial expressions that I imitated sent a message that *no one* could misinterpret.

2. **Observation activity**

Sitting around a table, take turns describing in three to four sentences the nonverbal behavior you observe in one of your relationships or someone else's (could be friends, co-workers, teammates—or characters from a book, movie, or TV show).

For example: *I notice that whenever Ben walks in the room, Jenna sits up straighter and can't take her eyes off him. I think he's aware that she's watching him, because he gets more boisterous. But he doesn't look over at her or ever talk to her. I think he likes the attention but doesn't seem to want to get to know her.*

Let the others ask questions to clarify what was shared in the observation. For example: *What do you mean by "he gets more boisterous?" Why do you think Ben doesn't look over at Jenna? Do you think Jenna's posture and watchfulness means she likes him? Could it mean something else?*

When you first start this activity, you'll probably have to come up with the initial example yourself. But once your child catches on, it becomes a very insightful and interesting activity. The questions can point out when there may be nuances in words, actions, or body language that could be misinterpreted or perceived differently by other listeners. In addition, you'll learn a lot of information about the various relationship-oriented contexts within which your child might be experiencing confusion.

Why Miscommunication Occurs

We all strive to communicate well and do our best to make sure that the message received by the listener matches the message we intended. Still, miscommunication plagues many of our interactions, even in love relationships. Typically, miscommunication occurs for three reasons:

1. There may be a discrepancy between what you say (your words) and how you behave (your facial expression or other nonverbal messages). When a discrepancy like this does occur, the truth usually lies in our behaviors rather than our words! For example, have you asked your child if they've done their homework, and they answer "yes," but they fidget and won't look you in the eye? It is hard to communicate effectively when someone's words say one thing, but the body language signals something else.

2. You may have trouble saying what you mean. You might be distracted because you're looking at your phone, thinking about something else, or watching your favorite program on TV. Psychologists have found that "noise," or outside distractions, that interferes with the speaker sending a message will result in the receiver incorrectly

hearing what was intended. Think how ineffective conversations are when they're held in a noisy bar, a rowdy sports event, or when you don't want to have the conversation at that moment. Similarly, if your child is looking at their phone or texting a friend, they aren't very good at telling you about what is on their mind or what they did that day.

3. The receiver can misinterpret the message or information delivered by the speaker for a number of reasons, such as when the receiver doesn't understand the speaker's frame of reference (can't relate), feels resentment or any other strong emotion toward the speaker (can't focus), or is more interested in asserting their own opinion on the topic than hearing the speaker's viewpoint (can't let someone else have the floor). It can also happen because the listener is distracted. Often, this third type of miscommunication is attributed to ineffective listening on the part of the receiver. I'm sure all of us, at some point, have been in conversations where we are more focused on what we want to say rather than on what's being said to us. This tendency to not hear what a partner or friend is saying is a big factor in miscommunication.

EFFECTIVE COMMUNICATION STRATEGIES

The goal of good communication is to accurately transfer a message from speaker to listener. In order to do that, the speaker must clearly say what they mean, and the listener must actively listen and receive the message that was sent. The good news is that we all can learn skills to improve the accuracy with which we send messages and with which we listen to the information being delivered. Both roles are *critical* to good communication and to your child's happy, healthy love relationships.

Relationship Advice in Action

"Communication is very important—like the glue that holds it all together." —*relationship survey response*

You can help your child learn these skills in two ways. First, you can model the effective communication strategies below. The more they observe you incorporating these skills (as a speaker and as a listener; with them in interaction and observing you interact with others), the more they are likely to use the strategies in their own lives. Second, you can directly share these strategies and their usefulness with your child, whether they seek out your advice or you bring up the topic yourself (I discussed how to start these conversations in Chapter 2). This is an essential conversation to have with your child, now and many more times in the future. The following strategies will never lose their importance in relation to your child's healthy, happy relationships.

Effective strategies: How to say what you mean

There is an art and a science to sending a clear message to someone. At first, it will take some practice and you'll consciously have to ask yourself:

- "Am I clear in what I just said?"

- "Could my friend or partner misinterpret what I just said?"

In time, the strategies and ways to say what you mean will become more natural.

Here are six strategies to help you (and your child) more effectively send information when communicating. There are real costs to a relationship—and all future relationships for your child—if we are not clearly understood.

1. Don't get distracted. You want to be focused on communicating. If you want to make sure that your message is clearly stated and delivered, ditch all distractions and give the conversation your full attention.

2. Don't engage in what I call "kitchen sinking." This is when you bring up all of the problems or issues ("everything but the kitchen sink") that have accumulated over time into the conversation. What can happen is that you begin with something that happened yesterday, and before you know it, you are moving on to issues from last week or last month. If you stay focused on a single issue or topic, it's much easier for your listener to understand and talk with you.

3. Do use "I statements" rather than "you statements." I statements start with "I" and then describe a distinct, specific emotional reaction or behavior. They take responsibility for *your* feelings and actions. You statements put the listener on the defense. Try saying, "I feel upset when you come home and go straight upstairs," rather than, "When you come home, you should talk to me before you go upstairs."

4. Don't use absolutes, like the words "never" or "always." These irrefutable and general comments are confusing to a listener because nothing is always or never something (e.g., "You're never on time when you have an appointment").

5. Do be mindful of your nonverbal communication components. Since nonverbal communication patterns convey meaning to a listener, and both the nonverbal and the verbal message together can either confuse or add information to what you are saying, be aware of your paralanguage (tone of voice), body language, facial expressions, and proximity to each other.

6. Don't expect that your partner knows how you're feeling about something. Clients often tell me they assume others should know when they're upset by looking at their expression, noticing their posture, or sensing their mood change. Don't assume others can read your mind. If you want someone to know something, just say it. Be direct.

Effective strategies: How to be a good listener

In addition to saying what you mean, good communication also requires that you listen well to what was said. Many people think they're already great listeners. But being empathetic is not the same as being an active listener. Active listening is a conscious behavior that requires more than your ears. It uses your eyes, your body, and your mind. You need to be able to really hear what your partner or others you care about are saying to you.

Relationship Advice in Action

"[The one quality I would like in a relationship for my children is] the ability to listen with an objective heart and mind." —*relationship survey response*

Here are six strategies to help you (and your child) more effectively receive information when communicating in close relationships:

1. Do paraphrase what you hear. Repeat what your partner said to you, in your own words. Give your partner a chance to agree that what you heard is what they actually meant. For example, "It sounds like you want to go to the party tomorrow night but you're unsure if you'll be comfortable there."

2. Do check out feelings. Ask your child for clarification about what they're feeling. Sometimes anger is really frustration, or regret is really sadness. Emotions can easily be misinterpreted. Ask for specifics. For example, "Are you worried or concerned about the exam tomorrow?"

3. Do validate and respect other people's point of view. You don't have to agree with their opinion, but it is important that you allow them their own feelings. For example, "I understand that work is stressful" or, "I hear you and understand that you're feeling lonely."

4. Do make listening a priority. Stay away from distractions. You can't do two things at once and do them well.

5. Do listen with your entire body. The way to show someone you are listening to what they are saying is to make eye contact, nod your head, turn your body towards the speaker, and lean forward rather than away.

6. Do be considerate and stay calm. When you're irritated and upset, you can't be calm. By staying cool when you're provoked and being able to calm down when you begin to get angry, you are mastering very valuable listening skills (see sidebar, Simple Tips: Four Ways to Stay Calm While Communicating).

SIMPLE TIPS: Four Ways to Stay Calm While Communicating

It is challenging to remain calm while you're communicating with a partner, child, or person close to you. Sometimes things are said that can provoke, hurt, or annoy you. Here are four strategies to help you stay calm and composed.

1. Avoid the temptation to attribute hostile intent. Start out by giving the benefit of the doubt. Ask yourself: Why are they having a bad day? What has changed in their life? Is there something that provoked them? Most of the time, confrontational behavior is because of something they are dealing with and has nothing to do with you.

2. Don't trade sarcastic insults when you get angry. Instead, take a "time out." Say, "I'm really angry right now; can we get a glass of water and continue in a minute?" Or, "Honey, I know you're upset right now. I understand. I love you. How about if you take some time and we can talk about this again later tonight/tomorrow?"

3. Take six long, slow, deep breaths to help yourself calm down. Taking in some fresh air also is a way to calm the emotions.

4. Follow up the next day. Set aside time to discuss how each of you is feeling, making sure to give attention to any lingering resentment or issue.

Describing the dos and don'ts of effective communication strategies all at once with your child can be overwhelming and you could be relaying more information than is applicable at that moment.

Instead, you may choose to share a specific speaking or listening strategy when an occasion calls for it. For example, children often use absolutes when they're upset or when they accuse a family member of a wrongdoing. When you hear them use "never" or "always" statements (i.e., "You never let me do what the other kids' parents let *them* do!"), point out how these words are an exaggeration that takes away from their real message, and that making these kinds of accusations can do potential damage to a relationship.

A teacher friend of mine, who often has to facilitate conflicts between her fifth-grade students, posts "Rules for Respectful Talk" on the classroom bulletin board that describe many of these same speaking and listening strategies. For each rule, she assigns a catchphrase, such as "Stay calm," "Face to face," "No interruptions," and "Speak your thoughts." The students soon learn the protocol for "speaking their thoughts" well enough that just the phrase prompts them to follow the rule. You can create your own catchphrases for each one. For example, a funny catchphrase for "don't kitchen sink" (bringing up all of the problems or issues into one conversation), might be "the kitchen sink is overflowing." When either you or your child says this phrase, it will prompt you to remember that strategy and stick to one issue at a time. These will become your own family's friendly (and hopefully fun) reminders when someone fails to follow the dos and don'ts to effectively say what you mean and listen to what is said.

REVIEWING THE STRATEGIES THAT AFFIRM HOW HEALTHY RELATIONSHIPS REQUIRE GOOD COMMUNICATION

Communicating effectively to make sure we share and receive accurate information in our love relationships takes a potent combination of **choosing appropriate words** and paying attention to the **tone in** our voice and **what we do with our face and the rest of our body** when we talk or listen. Teaching your child to become attuned to the **verbal and nonverbal** components of communication, and **how to incorporate effective communication strategies** when speaking or listening in their conversations can fend off the types of miscommunication that can harm their relationships. Help your child to understand that, by being mindful of the way they communicate, they can experience healthier relationships!

Recap

Two Types of Communication

- Verbal communication relies on language, and the specific words we speak (or write) are vital in conveying the message we want to transmit.
- Nonverbal communication can be more telling than our verbal communication, and involves paralanguage (tone of voice), body language, facial expressions, and proxemics (proximity to one another).

Why Miscommunication Occurs

- The main reasons for miscommunication involve: a discrepancy between what you say and how you behave; not saying what you mean because of distractions or evasion; and misinterpretation of the message between the speaker and the receiver.

Effective Communication Strategies

- Sending a clear message takes an intentional focus to make sure you: ditch the distractions; stick to a single topic; use

"I statements" to own your feelings; refrain from words like "never" or "always"; stay mindful of your nonverbal communication; and avoid making assumptions about what others perceive.

- Becoming an active listener so you can accurately receive information involves: paraphrasing what you heard; clarifying and respecting the other person's feelings; refraining from distractions; using attentive body language; and remaining calm.

CHAPTER 5

Manage the Battles: Keys to Handling Stress and Conflict

I was raised in Minneapolis, Minnesota, the oldest of three children. My brother and sister are three and five years younger than me, respectively. My father is a psychiatrist and my mother a teacher and family counselor. With parents who were so actively involved in the mental health arena, my childhood was full of trying to understand relationships, the many whys and hows of various behaviors, and how to effectively manage stress and conflict to maintain a healthy lifestyle, as you can imagine. My parents talked often with us about the negative health implications of too much stress and the benefits of addressing conflict in relationships. Not surprisingly, my siblings and I all ended up working in the health or psychology professions.

When I was very young and my father would return home from work in the evening, the three of us would run to the door screaming and shouting as soon as we heard the doorknob turn, racing to see who could get to my father first. He would calmly walk in and, with a peaceful composure, say hello and kiss the three of us. But before we could tell him our news from the day, he and my mother would go into the living room and talk for about 10 minutes—alone. Afterward, my father and mother would appear together, relaxed and ready to face our commotion.

I always found this very frustrating and didn't understand why my father wouldn't stop and speak with us, his three children. What did he and my mother discuss together on their own? Why weren't we allowed to come talk with them? Later, when I was older, they explained that their 10 minutes was the time they used to connect and talk about their days to each other—before family time. My brother, sister, and I were impatient, loud, and competitive with each other, and this time was their own to de-stress, cope with any issues, and regroup together. This short, private conversation was how my parents dealt with their stress and the chaos of three young children.

My parents haven't changed. They deal with stress and conflict in their relationship in the same manner. Married to each other for 60 years, they calmly discuss disagreements whenever conflict arises. I've never heard either of them shout, name-call, or be disrespectful to each other. Still, believe me, they have arguments and disagreements. When I was a teenager, I recall knowing precisely when my parents had a disagreement; they would talk more calmly and slowly and, instead of yelling, they would take a short break from each other until they were more composed and less irritated.

In the first four chapters of this book, I shared with you that making relationships a priority, initiating critical conversations, showing affirmation, and changing the way you speak are all important steps to help your child have happy, healthy love relationships. In this chapter I address how you can teach and model managing stress and relationship conflict in appropriate ways for your child. While I've discussed the importance of modeling healthy relationship behaviors in each chapter thus far, I particularly want to emphasize that the way parents model behavior in instances of conflict and stress is *especially* valuable for children. In highly charged situations where conflict or stress can upset their sense of safety or well-being, children look to their parents to see how to handle these tense situations. This is even true in instances when it's your child who is bringing the most stress and conflict into your life. I can't say it strongly enough: **It is *vital* for your child's relationships and health that you model healthy ways to deal with stress and conflict.**

Through investigating how stress and relationship conflict can take their toll, I'll share healthy ways to deal with both, and will give you specific tools to guide your child in managing stress and conflict in their lives, now and into the future. Whether we like it or not, our child *will* experience stress (which will affect their relationships) and they *will* have disagreements with the people they love, including you. We can't change that, so we must equip them with the tips and strategies to deal with life stress and relationship conflict. The research evidence is clear: People who resolve their conflicts constructively, and manage their stress well, experience more healthy, positive relationships.

MANAGING STRESS

You experience your own obstacles and challenges that create tension and anxiety in your life. These challenges, small and large, can stem from work, family, health, friends, or money issues. Perhaps you don't like the people you work with, or each month you face difficulties meeting your family's financial needs. Or maybe your mother and father continue to criticize you about your marriage or how you're raising your child. Whatever causes stress in your life, the single most important point to understand is that, in most cases, it is not what's out there causing the problem that makes your stress manageable or not, but how you think about it and react or respond to it! Your response is *key*—whether you maintain your composure or fly into a rage; whether you compartmentalize your stress or let it spill over into your relationships; and whether you relieve stress in healthy or unhealthy ways. The choices you make to manage your stress can add or detract from your well-being, that of your family, and your love relationship.

The same is true for your child. They'll experience times when they're unable to manage the changes or demands around them. Some causes of stress will be obvious—a grandparent dies, a friend excludes them from a clique, they break up with a girlfriend/boyfriend, they lose a job, or they don't get admitted to the college of their dreams. But you can't overlook the daily hassles and demands that contribute to their stress level—driving to school, having too much homework, competing on a sports team, rushing for a sorority or fraternity, studying for a physics exam, or going to the school dance. Over time, stress can accumulate and affect their relationships and their health. It can also influence how they treat and speak to you. The stress itself won't necessarily go away, but when your child handles their stress better using healthy coping strategies, it will help their love relationships and promote a healthier, happier relationship with you as well. Take time to talk to your child about these stressors, both big and small.

Make a point of examining three critical subjects. Depending on the age and personality of your child, you can approach these subjects when they are experiencing a big change (e.g., a breakup, a job loss, a health issue of a family member, isolation during the pandemic), dealing with a daily hassle or situation (e.g., studying for an exam, going on a first date, managing social media sites), or when the particular event or stressor is over and they have survived it.

1. **Who** can they reach out to if things get very demanding or stressful?

2. **How** can they identify the stressors in their lives?

3. **What** healthy coping behaviors are useful for dealing with stress?

Stress: Who can they reach out to?

Help your child determine who they can turn to for support and assistance in the family, their friend group, or community. Help them to understand that stress is common in people's lives. We all experience challenges and times when life becomes busy and demanding. Depending on their age, you might tell them about the stresses that you (or others) are experiencing—how you once had to make it work at the grocery store with little money, how your neighbor is trying to care for her ailing mother while working full-time, what your difficult boss demanded from you today, or the traffic you experienced on the way home. Share with them who you reach out to for help when you're feeling stress, and then ask your child to identify the people who might assist them if things get too stressful.

When my children were teens, we played the "help game." To play, draw five concentric circles, like a target. Then, help your child develop a list of five people they would turn to for help. Examples could include you, the other parent, a grandparent, sibling, other adult family member, love partner, friend, teacher, coach, counselor, neighbor, or the police. Put your child's name in the middle circle—the bull's eye—and then ask your child where they would place each name on the list in the circle that best represents how close your child feels to that person. The closer that person is to the middle, the closer your child feels emotionally to that person.

The placement will vary from child to child, and there is no correct way of putting the names on the diagram. Some children will have one or two people right next to them in the inner circle, and the other three people will be placed in the outer circles. Others will have all five people smack dab in the inner circle, since they feel close to all five people they consider their resources for times when they need some help.

The "help game" exercise has three functions:

1. It allows your child to identify who the people are they can turn to for help. This list can change over time as they grow older, but it will be useful for helping them handle stress by knowing they have people to turn to for help.

2. It reminds them that they can ask for help. They don't need to resolve or solve every challenge themselves.

3. It helps them understand that when people are emotionally close, they help and support each other. And the closer you feel to someone, the more likely it is that you will turn to them for assistance.

Stress: How can they identify stressors?

A second conversation to have with your child about stress is how important it is to identify the stressful triggers in their lives. Coping or dealing with stress is easier once they can identify what people or situations trigger stress for them (such as arguments at home, school homework, love relationship/friend issues, getting yelled at by a coach). A consistent finding in the research[18] shows that teenage girls report higher stress levels in their relationships than teenage boys. Most psychologists suggest that this difference is due to societal norms that emphasize the need for girls, and *not* boys, to be more sensitive to their social connections and more reliant on and empathic towards others. Girls then prioritize the connectedness and feelings of others over their own personal needs and desires, which increases their sensitivity to stress. While stress may land more heavily on girls' shoulders, discuss with *both* your daughters and sons how one's own needs, and those of others, need to be balanced, and how *not* to overlook their personal needs, desires, or feelings for those of others.

Try to help your child identify their stress triggers by having them fill out a stress journal for one week. Take a piece of paper and divide it into three columns. In the first column, have your child note which events and situations cause a negative physical, psychological, or emotional response for them. Have them write a description of what created the negative reaction. These responses could be in reaction to a person, situation, time of day, object, event, or even a thought they had. In the next column, have your child record the day and time for each stressor. In the third column, they should write how they felt at that moment and the intensity of that feeling. They could label their feelings with names of emotions, such as sad, angry, anxious, frustrated, bitter, rejected, or upset (these are just a few examples). The intensity can be labeled low, medium, or high. And finally, they should write what they did or said in response to the emotions, including behaviors such as cried, laughed, ate a lot, sweated, exercised, called my friend, said something mean back to the person, or breathed slowly and walked away.

This week-long stress journal allows you and your child (or your child on their own) to investigate their stress triggers. The journal will help them examine what types of events or people are causing stress in their lives and how they are responding to these situations. Are they coping in healthy ways or destructive ways? (More on this on page 137.) Did the stress triggers in their lives become fewer or greater as the week progressed? By grouping the stressors into common themes or similarities of events, people, or thoughts, your child can modify how they think about the stressors and how they react or respond to them.

I had a client whose 17-year-old daughter was a high achiever and put a lot of pressure on herself, to the point of experiencing nightly headaches. My client decided to try out the stress journal with her daughter. It quickly became apparent that a reoccurring

Stress Journal Sample Page

Negative event or situation	Day and time	How I felt and what I did
1. My boyfriend found my journal in my backpack when I wasn't looking and read about how I thought his parents were alcoholics.	Tuesday, 3:30 p.m.	**EMOTION:** I felt mad that he read my journal, but embarrassed that he saw what I thought of his parents. I also felt sorry for him because he's trying to cover up his bad home life. **EMOTION INTENSITY:** High **ACTION:** I told him my journal was private, and then said I was sorry for what I'd written about his parents. We didn't talk the rest of the night, which was uncomfortable. When I got home, I didn't want dinner that night and just went to bed early. I didn't finish my school homework.
2. A mean girl in my gym class yelled at me and pushed me against the wall when I accidentally tripped her.	Wednesday, about 11 a.m.	**EMOTION:** I got angry. I was also a little scared. **EMOTION INTENSITY:** Medium **ACTION:** I told her I hadn't meant to trip her, but that she'd hurt me. The teacher made her leave the gym. I wasn't sure what to do after that.
3. At soccer try-outs, my two best friends made the varsity team and I didn't.	Thursday, 5 p.m.	**EMOTION:** I felt sad, angry, frustrated, and nearly sick to my stomach. **EMOTION INTENSITY:** High **ACTION:** I rode home and tried hard not to cry. At home, I went to my room and cried the rest of the evening.
4. At the mall Diane stole some nail polish.	Saturday, 1 p.m.	**EMOTION:** I was mad. **EMOTION INTENSITY:** High **ACTION:** I told her it was wrong. I told her that I didn't want to hang out together anymore.

stressor was her last-period French class. The daughter was an excellent student and was accustomed to getting As in all her classes. But she felt apprehensive about her grade in Advanced Placement French. Her stress journal revealed that she became anxious just as class began each afternoon, and her anxiety remained at such a high intensity that she had a hard time concentrating. By the end of the class period, she usually had a pounding headache and wanted nothing more than to go home and hide out in her bedroom.

My client said that once her daughter could pinpoint her French class as the source of her daily headaches, she encouraged her daughter to talk to the teacher about her anxiety and fears about her grade. The teacher was able to reassure her daughter that she was doing well enough in class to earn a B, but if she felt that switching out of the advanced-level class would help her stress, she could do so and reevaluate whether to take the higher-level course the following year. Just identifying the source of her stress and knowing that she had options actually helped the daughter overcome her anxiety and headaches. She decided to remain in the class, and even raised her grade to a B+.

Stress: What are healthy coping behaviors?

When it comes to coping with stress, it is important to both model and discuss healthy ways to manage responses to stressful events. Parents who model appropriate ways to deal with stress are setting the stage for their child's ability to handle stress in healthy ways. Stay calm and remain patient, because when you respond constructively to your (or their) stress, you are better able to problem-solve for yourself or with your child.

Talk to them about healthy coping strategies for handling stress or challenges. The following are eight important tips for dealing with stress to discuss and model with your child:

1. **Exercise good self-care.** Proper nutrition, an adequate amount of rest each night, and some form of physical exercise are necessary for coping with and responding properly to life's demands and stresses. Self-care regimens are important. Also, don't forget to mention that "alone" time is essential to refuel and recharge their battery. Yes, friends are wonderful, but it is just as critical to schedule time to yourself, or "me-time."

2. **Focus on strengths.** Instead of dwelling on any weaknesses or what they don't have, focus on your child's strengths. As we discussed in Chapter 2, every child has gifts that make them special. Help your child identify what those distinctive qualities are, such as being a good writer, musician, athlete, or dedicated community member. Use positive labels to help them frame themselves. This helps them manage stress, but it can also increase their self-esteem and give them more to offer in their relationships.

3. **Set realistic expectations.** As your child experiences disappointments and setbacks, it is critical that they don't take them personally. They can use the disappointment to motivate them to work harder or try another course of action, but the disappointment should not be viewed as a reflection of their overall sense of themselves. Help your child set realistic expectations for what they hope to accomplish. This may mean saying "no" to certain friends and activities or prioritizing their time for what they can get done daily. Oftentimes, stress results from having lofty goals or from comparing themselves to others in unrealistic ways.

4. **Learn how to relax.** People have different techniques for helping themselves to relax and to relieve stress or anxiety. Help your child recognize those activities they consider relaxing and learn how to incorporate them into their lives. Some children like to express themselves creatively through dance, music, drawing, gardening, or art. Other children like to exercise or play sports. Journaling, walking in nature, reading, and listening to music are also activities that young people often find relaxing.

5. **Celebrate small victories.** Help your child break large, formidable goals into smaller, more manageable ones. For example, if your child decides they want to eat healthier, instead of changing everything all at once (meals, snacks, eliminating certain kinds of foods, adding other kinds of foods), they might focus on eliminating sugary candy and desserts from their diet for one full week as a smaller, more achievable goal. Acknowledge and celebrate small gains and accomplishments along the way. If you can focus on the progress along the way, the path to each goal is shorter and less stressful. You can encourage your child to celebrate their small victories by putting notes, comments, or photos on the refrigerator or sending a text that says, "Congratulations on your accomplishment!"

6. **Talk it out.** Studies show that when people talk to others about what is bothering them, they're able to relieve their stress and cope more easily. They may not resolve the issue, but the mere act of sharing or confiding in someone else leads to a better attitude and ability to manage the stressor. It is helpful when children have a special friend or caring adult to confide in. Remind your child about

the "help game" described earlier in this chapter, and who they feel emotionally close to. Encourage them to voice their feelings (they can even use the stress journal discussed earlier in this chapter) rather than locking themselves away in their room to cry or ignore their homework and responsibilities.

7. **Get out and help others.** By helping others who are in need, your child learns to become less concerned with their own problems. Their personal challenges and stressors may suddenly appear trivial compared to those of the people they're helping. Talk to your child about finding an organization in the community that provides a service that interests them, and commit whatever time your child can offer. They'll feel good about helping others, and it will keep their perspective in check.

8. **Maintain a sense of humor.** Laughing can release stress. Recent studies[19] have found that there are both short-term and long-term benefits to laughing, particularly when people feel stressed. According to neuroscientists, the effects of laughter and exercise are very similar. Laughter raises the level of infection-fighting antibodies in the body, boosts the levels of immune cells, relieves pain, and increases the production of endorphins (the brain chemicals known for their feel-good effect).

CONFLICT IN RELATIONSHIPS

Conflict is also a natural part of any relationship. Even happy couples have conflict. It would be unreasonable to think that two different people with different viewpoints would never disagree. But *how* a person engages in or reacts to a conflict makes an enormous difference to the health of a relationship. Think about the last disagreement or argument you had with your romantic partner or spouse. Did you raise your voice? Did you cry? Did you say things you regretted afterward? And, most importantly, did your child hear anything harmful that was said during the argument? If you and your partner handle conflict consistently in a destructive manner—screaming, interrupting, yelling, or calling names—studies show that two outcomes are likely:

1. You are *more than twice as likely* to break up or divorce.

2. Your child's well-being and ability to resolve conflict in a positive way in their own relationships is affected.

Let's address each outcome separately, and then come up with some healthy conflict-resolution skills for both parent and child—and discuss how gender plays a role.

Conflict: The effects of conflict on relationships

It's a fact: The way couples handle or resolve their differences predicts whether they'll stay together. One of the most striking findings from couples in the EYM study was that conflict itself was not a predictor of happiness or divorce over time. Instead, it was *how the couples managed the conflict* that predicted divorce or relationship happiness. Those couples who dealt with arguments constructively were more likely to be together (and happy) over the long haul. Conflict is an inevitable part of romantic relationships. In fact, a lack of conflict means the couple is not dealing with the things that matter.

Many people believe that if two people are fighting or disagreeing with one another, there must be something wrong. But you shouldn't expect agreement within love relationships about everything. You and your partner are two different people with different families, backgrounds, and perhaps even different cultures and religions. How could you expect to agree on everything?

Relationship Advice in Action

"When my wife and I argue or fight about something in front of the kids, we tell them, 'Mommy and Daddy aren't mad at each other, we're just talking and communicating something passionately and we still love each other.' My wife and I believe, above all else, communication is a major part of a successful relationship." —*relationship survey response*

As I mentioned in the introduction, I was fascinated to find in my long-term study of marriage that the couples who said they *never* fought were actually more likely to divorce than those who accepted the inevitability of occasional conflict and had learned how to manage it in a constructive way. In a surprising finding from the study, when couples were asked if they had tensions or differences regarding six topics—money, own family, spouse's family, how to spend leisure time, religious beliefs, and children—those who said "no" to all six topics were also the couples who were not very happy over time. Couples could also voluntarily say, "We don't/we never disagree." Again, these were not the happy couples. The happy couples in my study who are still together after more than three decades readily admit that they disagree. But what makes happy relationships different from unhappy ones is that the partners learn how to deal with conflict in a healthy, productive manner.

Emphasize that disagreements are a normal quality of happy relationships. Working through a conflict thoughtfully and considerately with your partner can help you to better know each other and even improve your sense of intimacy. You don't have to agree, but it's important to listen to and respect your partner's point of view. Relationships of all kinds—not just romantic relationships—have disagreements and tension that, if handled calmly and respectively, can lead to happier and healthier connections. You can refer to page 125 in Chapter 4 for four strategies to help you stay calm and composed during disagreements.

Relationship Advice in Action

"While helping my daughter through a rough relationship I've passed on the tools I've learned to guide her. Most notably is how to argue healthy and fair with your partner." —*relationship survey response*

It is important to caution your child that, if another person ever becomes abusive during a conflict through words or actions, they need to protect themselves—physically and emotionally. They should immediately leave the room and, depending on the level of threat to their safety, leave the home or building and seek protection from a trusted friend or family member (or a law enforcement officer if they fear for their safety). Conflict and the airing of different perspectives never should come to the point of threats or inflicting harm on someone. Unfortunately, some people are ill-equipped to work through conflict and can lash out in anger. And sadly, some people use abuse as a way to exert power or control over others so they can feel better about themselves. This behavior is *never acceptable*, and if abuse of this sort ever occurs, counseling should be sought if the relationship is to continue.

Conflict: Its effect on children

The teenage years are often the time when conflicts and disagreements with your child increase in frequency and intensity, as your child develops a greater need for independence and autonomy. Rest assured, though; this is common. Studies show that conflicts between parents and children are most frequent during early adolescence, most intense during mid-adolescence, and then decline gradually thereafter.

SIMPLE TIP: How to Resolve Disagreements Respectfully with Your Child

If you and your child are disagreeing frequently, try using these phrases to work through conflict and avoid hitting a heated impasse:

- I understand what you're saying, but I disagree because...

- You sound angry; did I do or say something to upset you?

- That might be true, but could you be overlooking the possibility that...

- What experience have you had to give you the perspective that...

- I hear what you're saying, but my take on this is different because...

- Can we agree to disagree on the topic of...

In addition, as relationship demands change from early to later young adulthood, parents and children also change the way they resolve conflicts with each other, resulting in more positive problem-solving behaviors and conversations that are more egalitarian and balanced. These changes in conflict frequency, conflict intensity, and styles of conflict resolution are associated with greater well-being for children and parents.

The teenage years is also the time when children are most likely to carefully observe the relationship traits and behaviors of their parents. It is the time when children begin to see themselves in partnership with others. And, when children live in a household where adults are consistently cold, angry, and conflicted toward each other, they are affected. If parents regularly say mean or cruel things about each other in front of children, this creates even more anxiety and unhappiness. Persistent, unresolved, negative conflict may lead children to feel responsible for the parental struggles, even if they aren't the cause or the source of the conflict.

Research by sociologist Paul Amato[20] finds that when parents fight with each other in a hostile, acrimonious, and spiteful way, their children experience more anxiety, worry, and nervousness. As you'd expect, children are happiest and better off when their parents are respectful and cordial, even if they disagree with one another. In several long-term studies, Amato has shown that parental conflict has adverse effects for children whether the parents live together or not. He has found that children are adversely affected even when ex-partners argue and have conflict with each other after divorce. In addition, Amato's research shows that children are worse off (emotionally and psychologically) when parents *don't* divorce and they must live amid frequent parental conflict and disagreements.

Relationship Advice in Action

"I discussed with my kids that moms and dads don't always agree, but this doesn't mean they don't love each other. Parents can have a disagreement and it doesn't involve the children." —*relationship survey response*

Dealing with conflict in a healthy and constructive way is vital for your child to observe and learn, whether those interactions are between you and them, you and their other parent, or you and your love partner.

Conflict: Healthy resolution skills

There's a common misconception that fighting should be done behind closed doors, but you need to have conflict in front of your child if you want them to have happy, healthy relationships. When I was first married, my husband and I did all our fighting upstairs at night in the bedroom. My children never saw that two people who love one another could have a conflict. One day, my husband and I were disagreeing in front of our children about what television program to record and my son thought we were going to get a divorce. We explained to him that our relationship was like all relationships— we disagree sometimes but we try to resolve the conflict respectfully. Conflict and disagreements can happen between two people who love one another, but that doesn't mean we're getting divorced. We also made it a point after that to disagree in common areas of the house more regularly.

If your kids don't see you having conflict and handling it constructively, they may grow up thinking that people who love each other don't disagree or have conflict. Then, when they have conflict with their own partner—and fight they will—they'll assume the relationship is in trouble and run from it, even if it's an exceptional, healthy relationship.

In a good love relationship, couples are able to handle conflict constructively: they fight fair, know when to engage in an argument or to let it go without resentment, avoid name-calling, validate each other's feelings, and remain calm when talking. The key to "healthy conflict" is in how you treat one another when you're at odds. Also, bear in mind that the way you behave now when you have a disagreement will likely remain how you will (or won't) resolve problems in the future. The patterns for how you react to disagreements tend to be set at an early age, so it's even more vital to start conversations with your young adult child about how to resolve conflict if you haven't already.

Although this chapter focuses on helping your child develop healthy conflict-resolution skills, one troublesome conflict pattern is worth sharing. Marriage researcher John Gottman has studied relationship conflict for many years.[21] He studies couples by asking them to discuss a recent disagreement with each other in his laboratory. He then carefully investigates the resulting interactions between the two partners.

Gottman has found that couples who fail to maintain a five-to-one ratio of nice behaviors to nasty behaviors when conversing with each other are more likely to break up over time. "Hostile couples" use a great deal of criticism, contempt, defensiveness, and withdrawal when disagreeing with each other. In other words, they are detached, uninvolved, and snipe at one another as they converse. According to Gottman, this conflict style is volatile, destructive, makes the existing disagreement significantly worse, and leads to unhappiness in a relationship.

For Gottman, the key to healthy conflict resolution is not the amount of conflict you have with your partner, but the ratio of positive to negative exchanges. As long as romantic couples maintain a minimum of five positive exchanges for every one negative, couples can have conflict and not damage their relationship.

Helping your child develop healthy conflict resolution skills will make a tremendous difference in the health of their love relationships down the road. Scrutinize the way in which you and your partner deal with conflict and whether the behavior you display is how you want your child to settle their own disagreements. Talk with them not only when you are trying to resolve your own conflicts, but as you observe other conflict-resolution behaviors when you come across them—between family members, on TV shows, or out in public.

> ### Relationship Advice in Action
>
> "[The one quality I would like in a relationship for my children is] the ability to get through conflicts in a healthy and mutually helpful way." *—relationship survey response*

The following are five helpful tips to fight fairly when you have a disagreement:

1. **Calm yourself with a break.** If you feel yourself getting really heated up, don't storm off without explanation. It's okay to take a break as long as you tell the other person that you're going to come back soon to finish the discussion. This means a break of seconds or minutes, but not hours. As we discussed in Chapter 1, the brain can't effectively problem-solve when you're extremely upset and emotional and needs at least 30 minutes to calm down and return to normal functioning. Remember the four strategies to help you stay calm and composed that that can be found on page 125 in Chapter 4.

2. **Timing is everything.** It's important to pick a time to deal with hot-button topics when you can be alone together with no distractions. Don't confront the other person with the problem that's been troubling you as soon as they walk in from work, and definitely not at night or in the bedroom. This is a very important note: You never

want to associate the bedroom with arguments and conflict with your love partner, *so step out of the bedroom.* Emailing, texting, and phoning are perfectly acceptable ways to initiate prickly conversations—to set up a time to talk later on—but not for having the discussion, which needs to be face-to-face. Walking and talking is also a great option, especially for men. Research finds that communication is easier for men when they're engaged in an activity.

3. **Don't name-call.** Remember that there are always multiple ways of conveying your message. Even if the conversation is a difficult one, don't use any name-calling when you talk to one another. I always recommend starting with a positive comment ("I really appreciated your help with the grocery shopping yesterday") before you get to the hard stuff ("I understand that my mother can be difficult and demanding, but I don't feel like you treat her with respect").

4. **It's okay to stay away from taboo topics.** As anyone in a relationship knows, there are always a few topics that you may not be able to resolve with the other person. These are called "taboo topics"—issues that you will never agree on or that are perpetual sources of conflict. Taboo topics are okay (e.g., religion, politics, the timing of your future grandchildren), as long as you don't have *too* many taboo topics and the topics aren't significant to your day-to-day lives or your future together. Sometimes you can work these differences out, reach a compromise, or agree to disagree.

5. **Focus on what you can change.** When you tell the other person what annoys or irritates you, don't attack their perceived character traits ("you're irresponsible;" "you're

messy"), but rather, focus on changeable actions ("I get upset when you forget to call me on my birthday"; "I get annoyed when you throw your clothes on the floor"). People are much better at changing their behaviors than their personality flaws. Also, it is important to focus on what *you* can change—which in most cases is your reaction or response.

Set ground rules within your family about what behavior is acceptable and what crosses the boundary of civility. For example, a close friend of mine has a son and daughter, both in high school, and, like many siblings of that age, their interactions sometimes disintegrate into teasing and other types of provocation. Unwilling to play referee, my friend tends to let them have their spats, but she has laid down rules the children know they're not allowed to break without consequences. Specifically, the teenagers aren't allowed to use hurtful language or hurt each other.

Once, as we walked together from a restaurant to our cars, the teenagers began arguing with each other, and the boy yelled at his sister: "F*** you! I hate you!" The mother immediately turned, and calmly asked her son to walk with her to a patch of grass near the restaurant. My friend talked with her son, and you couldn't even tell she was upset. Her son knew he'd crossed the line, and he was appropriately remorseful. The daughter and I went to the cars, where we waited. When the son and his mother joined us a short time later, he apologized to his sister. My friend reminded both children, "We don't swear or use the "F-word in our family." By setting limits, she was instructing them in appropriate and inappropriate behavior to use in an argument.

Conflict: Relationship conflict and gender

My EYM study on marriage finds that in general men and women process conflict, arguments, and disagreements in fundamentally different ways. Women are much more sensitive than men to conflicts and problems that arise in their relationships. When a woman has a disagreement, it lingers in her mind for two to three days. She replays it over and over, analyzing the details of the disagreement. Following an argument, she wants to go over it again the next day. Women like to feel as if any conflict in their relationship is minimal and manageable, and part of that is discussing the whys and whats of a disagreement.

Not so with men. When men have a conflict with their partner, once the discussion has taken place, they consider it resolved. The fight doesn't linger in their minds, and they've moved on to thinking about something else. In fact, when the woman comes up the next day and says, "Can we talk more about what we were discussing last night?"—he may have no clue what the fight was about! This can be infuriating to women until they learn that men simply "do" arguments differently than they do.

Studies of young adults also show that there are gender differences in how problems are handled in interpersonal relationships, whether that tension occurs at school, at home, with friends, or in their own love relationships. Adolescent boys and young men use a problem-focused style of managing differences or disagreements, where they focus on how to solve the problem so that it goes away. If boys or men seek help from others to manage the conflict, they look for what psychologists call "instrumental support," whereby the help or assistance will fix or solve the problem. In these instances, they want concrete feedback and validation during the problem-solving process.

In contrast, teen girls and young women tend to avoid using conflict strategies that might harm or jeopardize their relationships with others. They focus on making the situation better, and often seek support or advice from others, while expressing their concerns and emotions. If they do seek help from others to manage problems, they want what psychologists call "emotional support," the kind of help characterized by empathic or comforting feedback.

Take the case of two good friends who are boys. One of them, Dylan, likes a girl, Claire. But Claire asks Dylan's good friend, Jason, to a school dance. Jason would like to go to the dance with Claire, but he wonders if he should decline for Dylan's sake. When Jason solicits advice from other guy friends about what to do, he wants them to focus on the pros and cons of going to the dance with Claire. He needs his friends to tell him what to do, not sympathize with him. They all tell him to go with Claire, since she asked him. Jason then tells Dylan that Claire asked him to the dance, and that he'd like to go. Dylan tells him to go ahead and go, and that he won't hold it against him.

If the same scenario happened with two close girlfriends, the outcome could be the same, but the process would be different. If Sadie liked Joe, but Joe asked Sadie's friend, Nicole, to the dance and Nicole really wanted to accept Joe's invitation, chances are Nicole would ask others *not* what she should do as much as what others think would be the emotional toll the situation could take on all involved. Nicole also would look for others to talk to who could sympathize with her predicament and give her feedback that it was a challenging situation. Depending on the strength of her relationship with Sadie, she may ultimately choose to turn Joe down and not betray a close friendship.

Understanding this fundamental difference in how girls and boys resolve differences or handle problems can be helpful in advising your child. While you may want to offer emotional support to your son, or provide instrumental support to your daughter, they may be searching for a different kind of feedback.

REVIEWING THE KEYS TO MANAGING STRESS AND CONFLICT

Equipping your child with the tools and strategies to deal with life's stressors and relationship conflicts **constructively** will help them to experience healthier, more positive relationships. Most people handle stress, conflict, and disagreements in the same way as their parents. This means that you must model **healthy strategies** to manage stress and relationship conflict. Let your child know that in most cases, it is not what's out there causing the problem that makes their stress manageable or not, but **how they think about it and respond to it** that matters most! Plus, the key to "healthy conflict" is in **how you treat one another when you're at odds**. This will ensure that they can deal with any conflict that occurs in their relationships in healthy, affirming ways.

Recap

Handling Stress

- Help your child examine:

    1. Who they can reach out to in times of stress.

    2. How to identify stressors.

    3. What healthy coping behaviors to use for dealing with stress.

Conflict in Relationships

- Since children learn much of their conflict-resolution skills from observing how their parents handle conflict, parents need to scrutinize their ways of dealing with conflict and decide whether the behavior they model is how they want their children to settle disagreements.

Relationship Conflict and Gender

- Women are more sensitive than men to conflicts and problems that arise in their relationships and tend to need more discussion around the issue than men.

- Boys and girls resolve conflict and problems differently: boys tend to focus on how to solve the problem so that it goes away, while girls want to focus on how not to harm or jeopardize their relationships with others.

CHAPTER 6

Bring the Topic of Money Out into the Open

In my high school, there weren't any classes on how to manage money, write checks, or identify savings opportunities for later in life. In all my years of formal education, I never learned how to talk about money or finances with other people. My teachers and professors never broached the subject, and my friends and I never sat around discussing what money meant to us growing up, whether we were generally savers or spenders, or how money figured into our future in terms of what we wanted to do or be.

In my family, the situation was completely different. My father and mother talked about money all the time: their salaries, how much money they saved and in what kinds of funds, their views on saving and spending, and how much of the family income went toward specific expenses. When I was a teenager, this information seemed to go in one ear and out the other. I vividly remember going on a walk with my father one day and discussing the mortgage for our house, the household expenses, and my father's savings plans for the future. I listened to what he said, but I wouldn't have understood—or cared enough to ask about—the concepts behind these finances. At the time, I wasn't interested in talking about money and finances, and I most likely didn't hide my disinterest.

But now, I recognize that the money conversations I had with my parents made a difference. Not only did they shape my views and approach to money, but they also had a large impact on my future relationships. Not surprisingly, I married a man who is very financially smart, competent, and stable. My husband also enjoys and is comfortable talking about money and finances with me. I also bring the topic of money out into the open with my young adult children, like my parents did for me.

In previous chapters, I shared five steps to help your young adult child have happy, healthy love relationships: practicing relationships as a priority, laying the groundwork for important conversations about relationships, appreciating their unique special qualities, changing the way you speak, and managing stress and conflict. In this chapter, I will discuss how having conversations with your child about money can significantly affect their love relationships. You will learn how issues with money start early in life, how to explore the meaning of money with your child, and strategies for financial discussions with them. You will also discover how it is critical to help your child gain concrete information about how money works and to learn smart strategies to save it, both of which can increase their attractiveness to partners and lead to better relationships over the long term. The goal is to help your child gain the necessary skills to effectively communicate about money and successfully manage it in their relationships. And the outcome is that they'll be happier and more satisfied in their love relationships.

ISSUES WITH MONEY START EARLY IN LIFE

It is fascinating that money is always welcome in our bank accounts but is not always a welcome subject to discuss. My research has found that in the early years of a marital relationship, money is the *number one* source of conflict between spouses. Even after a relationship matures, money issues tend to stick around. *Seven out of ten couples say that money causes tension in their relationship.* Studies[22] also show that money-related conflicts are more intense, last longer, are more likely to persist unresolved, and **have greater implications on a relationship than any other issue.** Couples avoid talking about money with each other because they fear the negativity, and when the topic does arise, it is typically because there is a financial situation that needs to be resolved—an overdrawn notice on a bank account, an expensive repair, or a disagreement about spending—reinforcing the perception that conversations about money will be tense, at best.

In most families, money isn't something parents generally talk about in front of their children. Research[23] shows that many parents think it is taboo to talk about financial issues with their children, and most avoid discussing money even with their adult children. Although developing a working knowledge of finance isn't something we generally acquire on our own, parents often avoid the topic entirely. Because of this, when money issues arise in our relationships (and they inevitably will with friends, romantic partners, and family), it becomes difficult to discuss and often leads to conflict.

Relationship Advice in Action

"[I learned from] my ex-husband how important money is for stability." —*relationship survey response*

To make matters worse, money is glamorized in the media, from billionaires and their opulent lifestyles to game shows where contestants compete for million-dollar prizes. Rarely do the realities of how to go about earning money, budgeting for expenses, or saving and investing appear as topics of mass appeal. We lack role models—particularly of the celebrity variety—who can teach us how to manage money and "talk money."

Society treats money as taboo

Where do our issues with money come from? For starters, in our society, money—how we manage it, save it, and spend it—is a taboo topic. Typically, parents don't discuss money issues in front of their children, friends don't share financial woes and salaries with each other, and love partners don't often reveal their personal financial challenges or hardships before they become financially entwined. Can you imagine someone on a first date asking the other person about their credit score, the balance remaining on their credit card, or how much debt they had accrued in the last few years? I don't think so! It would be considered the height of indiscretion.

In fact, love partners often don't broach the subject of debt, assets, and credit scores, even when they plan to marry or form a life commitment. In a National Foundation for Credit Counseling survey,[24] nearly 70% of adults said they had negative feelings about discussing money with a fiancé, while more than 20% said the discussion would either lead to a fight, reveal unknown financial issues, or even cause them to break off the engagement.

On TV shows or in movies, it's rare for couples, family members, or roommates to talk about money. Besides, how would it translate when most of the viewing public doesn't have enough understanding of financial concepts to grasp the meaning? Can you imagine a sitcom in which one roommate asks another for a loan, and then the roommates negotiate the terms of the loan? Or a romantic comedy in which a couple moving in together discusses how they'd share the rent or mortgage? More than likely, the viewers would switch channels.

Families pass on perceptions of money

Another source of money issues in relationships results from the way in which money symbolizes different things to different people: power, control, security, self-esteem, and even love. The meaning we attach to money affects how we talk to others about it, whether we're speaking with our love partner, friends, child, or parents. Too often, conversations between two people about money have little to do with money itself and more to do with the underlying personal meanings of money or other issues between the two people. Money is a tangible part of a relationship, so it is easy to project emotional issues onto concrete money matters. For example, if financial concerns have been a source of stress for you or if your family growing up didn't have extra money to spend, it is possible that you view money as essential to your security and stability. You think it is important to save for emergencies, and when you can't make ends meet or debt becomes unmanageable, you become very worried. Spending money on anything your child or partner may not necessarily need becomes a source of contention (between you and your partner).

It is important to be honest with yourself about how you feel about money. Also, think carefully as you discuss money with your partner/spouse, other family members, or friends when your child is within hearing range. How you view money and what it represents to you will most likely transfer to your child. If you've always been financially independent, for example, it may be hard for you to relinquish control of family spending. Your child may then learn that money symbolizes independence and control, and it is not a matter around which two partners join or work together. Or perhaps you've loaned money to a friend or family member, and that person hasn't made the effort to pay you back. When the outstanding loan starts to poison your relationship, it can be difficult to keep the grievances from trickling out in front of your child, who may begin to believe that money is a source of tension between people, and that it must be hoarded or stockpiled in order to feel secure.

Alternatively, you may like to take more risks with money and see it as a source of your self-esteem and confidence. The more money you acquire, regardless of the personal or relationship sacrifices, the happier and better you feel about yourself. You enjoy taking big risks with your money (e.g., investing in startup companies, initial public offerings, high-yield bonds) and you work hard to display your well-earned money by means of material things. In this instance, your child may begin to view money as a reward for hard work and as a symbol of how well they are doing in life.

What does money mean to you?

The way in which people approach money is often heavily influenced by the way they were raised. These influences can either taint their views toward money or help them have a healthy attitude about what money can and cannot contribute to their happiness. To help your child both understand the language of money and discuss money comfortably in their future relationships, it is important to first examine **your own views about money**. What does it mean to you? Before you talk to your child about the numerous perceptions people have toward money, you need to first figure out what it represents for you.

What does money mean to you? Ask yourself the following three questions:

1. **How did your parents deal with money?** Did your parents discuss money in front of you? Were your parents savers or spenders? Did they spend the majority of their money on themselves, their children, their possessions, or

their recreation? Did you see or hear your parents fight about money?

2. **What did money mean to you when you were growing up?** Was money something you took for granted because your needs were always provided for? Were your basic needs met? Did you receive an allowance? Did you work to contribute to the household or your personal expenses? On what did you spend money?

3. **How do you deal with money in your romantic relationships/marriage?** Do you and your partner/spouse have joint accounts? Are you responsible for your own expenses? Do you both contribute to the household? Do you ever feel constrained about spending because your partner won't approve? Are your relationships great when money is good, but terrible when money is tight? Are you honest with your partner about how much you earn, spend, and save? Is money tight in your relationship?

How to incorporate your attitude toward money when you talk with your child

Once you identify your own views toward money, you can more effectively discuss money with your child by acknowledging your own biases and explaining where you think they come from, based on your answers to the previous questions. Let your child know that people have different approaches toward money. Ask them what they think their approach would be and why. Remain nonjudgmental but point out the pros and cons to different ways of viewing money. Give it some time, then revisit the conversation to see how views change as both your own and your child's awareness grows.

In the next section, I will focus on what messages are important to get across to your child about money that will help them become more comfortable with handling their money and conversing with others about it. *Teaching your child to talk about money in their love relationships means that it is less likely to be a source of tension in their relationship, they are less likely to avoid talking about the topic entirely, and if conflict about money does arise in their love relationship, it won't have the same adverse effects.*

TALKING MONEY WITH YOUR CHILD

Of all the aspects of money that are important to communicate with your child, two stand out most. First, you want to give your child a basic comfort level for discussing money issues with others. Since society doesn't teach us how to talk about money, it is important that you talk about the issues that revolve around money and give your child a financial vocabulary.

I break this down even further by age group on page 167, but the more you share and model discussions of these topics (e.g., savings and checking accounts, tax brackets and withholdings, credit cards vs. debit cards, loans, compound interest, stocks and bonds, net income vs. gross income, and credit scores), the better they will be at talking about money in their relationships as adults. They will have the vocabulary to do so, and they won't fear that discussing money issues will lead to negativity and conflict.

When people don't talk openly about money, it can become a sensitive subject and lead to lasting conflict in a relationship. Open up the lines of communication on the subject with your child. Let them hear you talk about how you feel when you earn money, purchase something you really want, or have to pay the credit card bills. Use appropriate language (real words to describe what is happening) and teach them the correct vocabulary and definitions of those words.

For example, let your child see your tax return and tell them which tax bracket you fall into. You might use Tax Day (April 15) as an opportunity to explain tax brackets and withholdings. Show them your gross earnings and net income. When my daughter received her first paycheck, she was shocked at the amount of taxes deducted. Educate your child about taxes and withholdings, and, when the time comes, help them file their tax forms and determine if they'll receive a refund.

The second critical aspect is how finances work in our society (information is key!), and how to successfully manage money, both as individuals and in a relationship with shared expenses. Just as you want to give your child the interpersonal skills they need to become confident, capable members of society, you also need to give them the skills to attain financial awareness and independence. It's a tall order! They need to know how the income they earn must be budgeted to cover their expenses and pay back any debt. They need to understand the importance of saving for emergencies and retirement, and how investments can leverage their savings. And they should appreciate the importance of insuring against catastrophes, such as medical emergencies or car accidents. More details and the messages to convey to your child about these specific topics are covered later in this chapter.

Financial knowledge and the resourcefulness it creates have additional benefits to your child's future relationships. In talking with couples nationwide, I have found that when couples are financially responsible, it increases the romantic desire in their relationship. People who focus on "saving smart," or wisely planning for their financial future, are seen as more desirable than those who spend excessively, because savers are viewed as responsible, trustworthy, and more committed to the relationship.

SIMPLE TIPS: Appraising the Value of Money Clichés

The English language is rich with idioms and proverbs that refer to money. Write them down when you notice them and ask your child if they can explain what they mean.

To start you off, here are a few my favorites:

- Pinching pennies

- Money to burn

- Buyer's remorse

- Money doesn't grow on trees

- Hold the purse strings

- Another day, another dollar

- Lose your shirt

- Put your money where your mouth is

- Money doesn't buy happiness

- There's no such thing as a free lunch

Consequently, while lavish presents and expensive getaways are fun to daydream about, they aren't the most effective way to enliven a relationship or marriage. According to a Valpak Survey,[25] 74% of the respondents said they find people who save money responsibly more attractive. Besides sparking an attraction, being responsible with money can help couples sustain a long-lasting relationship. Sixty-nine percent of survey respondents considered learning how to save money responsibly together as a way to improve a relationship.

Five guidelines for talking about finances

Follow these five guidelines for providing general information about money with your child:

1. **Be honest about your view of money.** Describe how and why you formed your approach, and how it translates into your specific money behaviors (saving, spending, making certain purchases, emotions connected to the presence or absence of money, and your comfort level with discussing money matters).

2. **Be open-minded toward other approaches.** Emphasize that your approach to money isn't necessarily the right way, it is just your personal approach. Help your child recognize that people learn these meanings from society and from their family. Explain how cultural or social standards can lead people to have different perspectives on money.

3. **Talk regularly.** Sitting down and talking about money with your child is not a one-time discussion. Make a point of talking about money as a part of family discussions without always associating it with negative or challenging circumstances, even if your child is living out of the house or financially on their own. Share financial wins, too!

4. **Show how money decisions are made.** Explain how you handle money matters—whether at the grocery store, the bank, when you fill out your yearly taxes, or when you're balancing your checking/savings account. Moments when your child gets a first paycheck, fills out the FAFSA (Free Application for Federal Student Aid), applies for university financial assistance, or gets an apartment of their own

are good opportunities to discuss money concepts and financial planning.

5. **Set rules and limits.** If your young adult child still lives with you, come up with spending rules or limits together as a family. You could set a weekly budget and show how you track your spending. Discuss how you make decisions about what to purchase or not, given a specific amount of money. If your child is financially independent, use hypothetical situations to discuss spending rules and limits.

AT A GLANCE: Board Games That Teach Valuable Money Lessons

Board games are always fun family entertainment, and some are designed to teach important lessons about making, saving, and spending money. In addition, your young adult child can glean messages about the perils of reckless spending or the struggle to make ends meet after unexpected bumps in the road. The four games with money messages described below are among my family's favorites:

1. **The Allowance Game:** Appropriate for all ages, players earn money when they land on spaces with chores, like "walk the dog," and lose money on spaces like "pay for an overdue library book." They have opportunities to choose whether to spend or save their money.

2. **Pay Day:** The board is a month-long calendar and players must navigate through financial windfalls and pitfalls, including making decisions to save their money or take out loans, before getting to the end-of-month payday.

3. **Monopoly:** Players collect $200 with each revolution around the board. Meanwhile, they try to make wise investments in real estate, from which they can collect rent for added income.

4. **The Game of Life:** Players make a decision early in the game to pursue a college degree or go into a trade, and then see how that decision plays out as they move around the board, landing on a career, adding a family, and taking on additional expenses.

AGE-APPROPRIATE MONEY TOPICS TO DISCUSS WITH YOUR CHILD

Start talks about money topics early and broaden the discussion from values of money (as in denominations) to values (as in beliefs) around spending and saving money as your child gets older. Don't let their apparent disinterest discourage you, as the discussions can still leave an impression and provide a base of money knowledge. I've broken down money messages to communicate with your child by age below.

13–16 years old (or younger)

1. **How to earn money through work.** Discuss how we need money to buy things, and how we earn money through work. For example, describe your job to your child. When walking or driving through your town, point out the people working, like the bus driver or the police officer. Encourage your child to think about how they could earn money. Help them set up and advertise a neighborhood leaf-raking service or a pet-walking service.

2. **Deciding when to spend or save.** Help your child figure out how to *make choices* about spending or saving money. At this age, they understand the difference between "wants" and "needs." Once they begin to have a source of income (from babysitting or odd jobs, job, gift money, or allowance), consider no longer buying what your child wants for them, but having them save for the things on their want list. Also, discuss why sharing, or donating, to those in need or other charitable causes can help make a positive difference.

3. **Protect information online.** Talk about the dangers and costs of sharing information online. For example, make it a rule that your child does not give out personal information when on the computer and does not buy anything online without your permission.

16–18 years old

1. **Smart savings goals.** Show your child how to organize, manage, and keep track of their money. Discuss the general approach to smart saving. Help them set goals regarding how much they can save. Ask what they will have to give up in order to reach their goals and whether they think it is worth it. Saving for short-term goals, such as a bike or computer, as well as for long-term goals, such as a car or college, are both important. Parents and other adult family members can add to this savings as part of gift giving.

2. **How banking works.** Show your child how to write and record checks, use an ATM card, and how to balance

checking and savings accounts. Describe how interest works, and why starting to save early in life pays off through compound interest. Visit a bank or credit union and ask about the various accounts or funds for saving money, and the interest rates and penalties associated with the different accounts.

3. **Risks of credit and debit cards.** Describe the difference between a debit and a credit card, the importance of not overdrawing from their bank account when using a debit card, and the costs of not paying a credit card bill in full each month. Emphasize that using a credit card is like taking out a loan and if they don't pay the amount charged on their card each month, they'll pay interest on their purchases.

4. **Tax withholdings.** Explain why taxes are taken out of everyone's paychecks. Discuss the difference between gross pay (before taxes) and net pay (the amount they take home). Explain the W-4 form that every employee must fill out when starting a job, and discuss tax brackets.

5. **College costs and student loans.** If teens are considering a college or trade school education, have frank conversations about what you can afford. If your child plans to take out student loans to help pay for college, help them to understand the details around repayment schedules and what they can afford based on the salaries offered in the professions or trades they plan to pursue.

18+ years old

1. **How to borrow for large purchases.** Help your child understand how big purchases are made or paid for.

Explain how mortgages and loans work, their advantages and disadvantages, and how to shop for the best rates. Caution them about over-extending, and what can happen if they are unable to make loan payments.

2. **Insurance requirements.** Health, car, renters', and home insurance are often required by law. Currently, children in the U.S. can stay on their parents' health policy until the age of 26. Discuss with your child when you expect them to pay for their own insurance, and how they need to factor their insurance premiums into their budgets. Let them know that, before purchasing insurance, it is important to comparison shop and understand what the different policies cover.

3. **Investments and long-term savings accounts.** Highlight the advantages of putting some income into investments or accounts in which their money can grow, particularly IRAs or, if their employers offer them, retirement or 401(k) accounts. While loan repayment is often the first concern of young adults, educate your child in the language of investing—how to diversify investments, consider risk, and plan for large purchases, financial setbacks, or retirement.

An excellent reference for money messages for children by age, developed by the President's Advisory Council on Financial Capability, is the informational chart, "Money as You Grow: 20 Things Kids Need to Know to Live Financially Smart Lives."[26] It lists specific recommendations for what children should learn regarding money as they grow into adulthood.

THE MORE YOU KNOW: The pros and cons of giving child an allowance

The debate over whether parents should give an allowance to their child is ongoing. Consider the pros and cons below and weigh them based on what you experienced as a child, what you know now, and what is best for you and your child.

- Pro: Your child will receive money to save and spend on their own.

- Pro: If you require that your child earns their allowance based on chores or responsibilities around the home, they will understand how money is earned through completing assigned work.

- Pro: Your child will have money with which to learn how to make decisions about money management through their own trial and error.

- Con: Your child will expect to be paid for chores or fulfilling their responsibilities around the home.

- Con: Your child will recognize that doing things around the home is rewarded for some (children) and not others (parents).

- Con: Your child could apply this requirement for compensation when helping around the home in their love relationships.

DISCUSS WITH YOUR CHILD HOW MONEY ISSUES CAN AFFECT RELATIONSHIPS

As money conversations evolve to encompass how finances are handled in relationships, focus on messages your child needs to know to help them form happier, more stable love relationships. In my experience working with couples for the past three decades, I've uncovered two essential points for dealing with money *within* relationships:

1. The importance of **joint money decisions** with your romantic partner.

2. The importance of **not keeping money secrets** from your partner.

My EYM research revealed that both issues predict happiness and stability in relationships over time.

Topic #1: Make money decisions together

In my work with couples, I've found that it is not unusual for one partner to take on the primary role of managing finances. But you might be surprised to know that the role is not typically held by one gender or the other. In other words, if we are referring to a heterosexual romantic relationship, the primary money manager could be either the man or the woman. And it also doesn't depend on who earns money outside the household (or who earns more if both are employed outside the household).

Regardless of who runs the household finances, one EYM study finding is clear: **It is vital that both partners are involved in and aware of the finances.** My research shows that couples have less conflict when they share (or consult one another) in any important financial decision. When couples make financial decisions together, they are also more likely to stay together over time. Big financial decisions should *not* be made solely by the partner earning the most money. Even if partners have separate bank accounts, it is vital that each knows the other partner's assets and debts. Being knowledgeable about assets and debts together and separately is key. Of course, partners don't need to check with each other each time they eat out or buy new clothes. But, with any large-item purchases, they are better off consulting each other or making the purchase together. I encourage couples to agree on a threshold amount ($50, $100, $500—the amount will vary) that either partner can spend without consulting the other.

Talk to your child about the importance of both partners taking an active role in managing (or understanding) the family finances. Let them know that, in any healthy relationship, both partners should be aware of their household expenses, the amount going to savings, and what parameters they agree on around spending. Model these same behaviors in your own love relationship, so your child can observe what that means in practice.

Both partners need to feel that they are part of a team, regardless of whether their bank accounts are separate, joint, or a combination of the two. Partners can take on separate responsibilities when it comes to money—for example, one can pay bills and the other talk to the accountant—as long as both partners know what is going on financially, and both consult the other partner on all big purchases.

Topic #2: Don't keep big money secrets from your partner

Honesty with your love partner builds trust and intimacy—and we all value honesty in our relationships. We expect our partner to be completely honest and open with us, so when one partner has secrets or withholds information, it has a negative effect on the relationship.

When I asked the happy, contented EYM couples whether they felt their partners told them things that were not completely true, their answers differed significantly from those of struggling couples, confirming that honesty plays a crucial role in relationship happiness. Statistically, 78% of the happy couples said they "never" feel that their partners are dishonest about money, compared with 54% of the struggling couples.

What about "editing" for your partner's own good? Is telling a white lie about a purchase or spending habit okay? In my opinion, it is fine to protect your partner (or edit) regarding some types of information (e.g., maybe you'd prefer to keep the price of your hair salon visit a secret). But, if you hide or withhold *important* money matters (spending, earning, saving), the two of you can't grow as a couple. And, over the long haul, trust will fade (or won't ever develop) in your love relationship.

One of the questions I often get from couples about money involves whether it is a good idea to keep separate accounts, where each has money for individual expenses and purchases. Certainly, this can work, as long as there isn't financial secrecy. Separate accounts allow two people to have some financial independence, maintain a sense of autonomy, and not feel as if another has control over their every spending whim. Some couples keep just one joint account. Other couples have a joint account, along with separate accounts. Still others have separate bank accounts, with no joint account. These couples work out a plan regarding who pays what bills or makes which purchases. No one way is more suitable than another, as long as couples don't withhold or hide important money information from each other.

Talk to your child, particularly as they enter love relationships in which they are sharing finances, living together in one household, building assets together, or purchasing joint household items (or pets). Building financial trust with your partner requires consulting each other on important money matters and keeping them out in the open.

If your child doesn't feel that they can be completely open with their partner, ask them to think about three important themes:

1. How do you think your partner would feel about having the information kept from them? Would your partner say it is no big deal?

2. What if your partner withheld the same information from you? How would you feel? Would you feel hurt because there was a lack of trust or openness? Or would you think this was a small and unimportant issue, and you'd be fine with not knowing?

3. What is stopping you from being completely honest with your partner? Do you feel guilty, or do you fear their reaction? Sometimes, it is important to understand *why* you are reluctant to disclose the whole money truth, and then address that issue. Often, once you know why you're keeping the secret, it can be easier to open up about it.

Be sure to emphasize the idea with your child that openness and honesty in money issues have effects on the health of any romantic relationship.

REVIEWING THE VALUE OF TALKING ABOUT MONEY

Money issues play a **significant role** in the health of relationships. Unless parents help their young adult children feel comfortable talking about, and become knowledgeable about, managing money, they will struggle with their **own financial responsibilities** and with **handling finances in their relationships**.

Talks about Money Recap

Money issues can create conflict between love partners.

- Seven out of ten couples in the Early Years of Marriage (EYM) study said that money caused tension in their relationship.

- Studies show that money-related disagreements have greater implications for love relationships than other conflict topics.

- Couples don't know how to discuss money matters, and their conversations about money often take a negative turn.

- Couples who are open with each other about money matters and make big financial decisions together have a stronger romantic attachment.

Conversations about money are taboo in our society.

- Unless parents talk about money and finances, the child won't generally acquire the information they need to handle financial matters responsibly for themselves or as part of a couple.

- Parents pass on their own perceptions about money when discussing finances, and it is important that parents assess and address what money means to them.

- Provide the vocabulary to talk about money and teach your child the skills to attain financial independence.

- Guidelines for talking with your child about finances include: being honest about your own views of money; being open to different approaches to money; being willing to explore the topic often; being able to explain how to handle money matters; and being prepared to establish spending rules.

Start discussing money with your child at an early age.

- Understand which messages are appropriate to share at what age so that knowledge of money keeps pace with growing financial responsibilities.

- Talk with your child about the value of money (in terms of denominations) and broaden the discussion as they age to include values (in terms of beliefs and practices) around money.

Money matters can make or break relationships.

- Relate the importance of making large financial decisions together as a couple.

- Emphasize the fact that partners should not hide important money issues if they want to maintain trust in their relationship.

CHAPTER 7

Make a Big Deal about the Right Relationship

I moved to Ann Arbor in my late 20s to take a tenure-track professor position at the University of Michigan. I had lived in the Midwest my entire life, so the move wasn't that different or risky. At the time, I was single. I didn't know anyone who lived in Michigan, let alone in the city of Ann Arbor.

I consider myself to be a social extrovert, but I had been warned that the first few years of a professor position at the university would be challenging. The consistent message was that it would be difficult to date and join extracurricular activities because the job was demanding and time-consuming. And, although this next comment will date me, dating and finding love online was not popular at that time. I worried—how was I going to find my love partner?

My solution was to tell everyone I met that they had permission to set me up. I told my colleagues that I would go out on a date with anyone once. What did I have to lose? Well, I went on a lot of blind dates that first year in Ann Arbor. The stories and interesting people I met could fill a whole other book! It wasn't until I was invited to join a friend of mine, who was hoping to fix me up, at a religious event that I saw the man I would end up marrying. I never got to talk to him that day but I thought he had a wonderful smile and a confident look, so I told my friend, "Yes, please fix me up with him."

Well, that started a chain of events. It turned out that my friend was good friends with his sister. She told his sister that I was interested in meeting him. Even though he had never seen me, when he heard that I was in academia, he quickly said, "No thanks!" The world of academics wasn't his "thing." What changed his mind? His sister told him that, although I was a professor, I taught courses in human sexuality and relationships. Amazingly (smart man!), he changed his mind.

Our first date was in January, we were engaged in May, and we married in November of that same year. We knew we were right for each other because, even though we had our differences, our key life values were the same. We communicated extremely well, he was affirming and talkative, we were physically attracted to one another, and we handled stress and disagreements well.

The ways in which your child meets and connects with others are a bit different now. Further, given the COVID-19 pandemic, it is even more challenging for people to meet potential love partners. But what has remained the same are the benefits of being in a healthy love relationship, the experience of love, and the questions your child needs to ask to see if a relationship is right for them.

As discussed in Chapter 1, when your child is in the right love relationship, they're going to feel better and look better! In my research, I found that people in loving relationships experience less anxiety and depression, are better able to handle stress, are happier with life in general, and are motivated to take better care of themselves. When people are in the right relationship, the whole world seems more positive, and they feel better about themselves.

I'll never forget the story one of the women from a happy couple in my study told me about her love partner. She had recently had emergency surgery that required two nights and three days in the hospital. Not once did her partner leave her side. He even slept in a vinyl fold-down chair for two nights and didn't complain once. She explained that if it weren't for him and his hand-holding through unbearable pain and nausea, she *never* would have physically and emotionally survived that hospital experience. I always get very emotional when I remember that story.

In previous chapters, you learned that in order for your young adult child to have happy love relationships it is crucial for you to build trust and help set realistic expectations, lay the groundwork for important relationship discussions, show gratitude and appreciation, change the way you communicate, and bring money out into the open. In this chapter, we will discuss the top four ways for your child to meet love partners. You can share this information with your child if they're having challenges finding potential love interests and the right partner for them. I'll also be focusing on two kinds of love, how to distinguish love from lust, and ways your child can recognize if a relationship is right for them. Discuss what you learn in this chapter with your child as they start new love relationships. These discussions may not be easy—try to be patient; don't take resistance personally; continue to build trust, self-disclose, and give affirmations to your child; and remember to ask the right kinds of questions. The science-based information will help your child's relationships get off to a good start!

FOUR WAYS TO FIND LOVE PARTNERS

There are four top ways for your child to find that special someone: group activities that meet regularly, online dating, a matchmaker, and blind dates. Let's look at each of these dating methods, one by one, to understand why they work.

Join an activity that meets regularly

One of the top ways for your child to find the right love relationship is to join a group that meets often or to participate in a group activity on a regular basis, like a book club, softball team, or a religious group. Animal lovers could seek out a local dog park or sign their dog up for an obedience course. Your child could volunteer for a political cause or at a nonprofit organization. Any activity that involves meeting and spending regular time with people who have similar interests can set the stage for new love.

Studies[27] show that mere contact with a person (or repeatedly seeing someone) can increase how much you like that person, a phenomenon researchers refer to as the "mere exposure effect." For example, your first trip to a café or store may have been nothing more than a hello, a credit card swipe, and a dash for your car. But after a few trips, you may find yourself chitchatting with the barista or clerk, and they begin to know that you like a cappuccino with low-fat foam or that you like your items to be double bagged.

The same applies in the dating world. When your child participates in an activity on a regular basis, they'll feel more comfortable talking with and asking questions of the people who are there. When they already have an activity in common, they won't have to worry as much about finding a good opening line. One of my clients was attending a weekly book club at the local library. He noticed that there was a woman there who attended every meeting. She was energetic, asked questions, and loved to laugh. After a month, he went up to her to ask, "How did you like the last book?" The question was simple and the conversation didn't feel awkward. They have been dating ever since.

Join an online dating app

Second on the list of top dating strategies is to join an online dating app. I'm a huge advocate of online dating and it's with good reason. Research[28] shows that more than 40 million Americans turn to the internet or apps to find a love partner and one in five new relationships are formed between people who've met online.

Over the last few decades, online dating has become a successful way to meet someone who is compatible. This isn't by accident. Many online dating services hire researchers and psychologists, like me, to assist with how the sites are structured, how online profiles are developed, and how potential dates are matched and recommended by users. Online dating can expand the pool of potential partners, allow your child to cut to the chase quickly (they can message and chat with potential dates before meeting if they have the qualities they seek), and let them investigate several potential love interests at the same time and still have plenty of time for work, friends, and you!

These days, there are many dating apps and sites for every type of person. And it's all about your child finding the right site for them. They can ask their friends about their experiences with different apps, or you can research them together. Your child can join one site… or a few! One of my university students recently told me that she honestly doesn't know how she managed to date before she started the dating apps. She said that talking with people online cuts out the time, aggravation, and expense of all of those "first dates gone bad." Now, she is able to tell if someone might be right for her before they meet in person. As I discuss in Chapter 8, safety is an important issue to discuss with your children (see page 226), but this is true for both online and offline dating.

Hire a matchmaker

Third on the list of top dating strategies is to hire a professional matchmaker. There has been a rise in the number of singles who are hiring professional matchmakers to help them find potential partners. Matchmaking is ideal for your single child who is interested in taking a proactive approach to their dating life but is either too busy to search for dates or does not know where to meet quality singles. Matchmaking also serves as a solution for singles who are concerned with their privacy and security, something which online dating cannot always guarantee. One of my clients hired a matchmaker because he was exhausted and frustrated with the dating apps. He was also an extremely busy professional who started his own company. He was matched with several women who fit his criteria and qualities. He went out on a handful of dates, but when he met Alexandra, they felt like they had known each other for years.

Rest assured that professional matchmakers are not matching singles up with just anybody. Most matchmakers today are trained and accredited by institutes (e.g., The Global Love Institute) that teach them best practices and procedures. After a personal consultation to get to know your child, the matchmaker will work to find the best matches for your child. When you hire a matchmaker, they find, screen, and interview all potential dates. That way, the singles your child meets with have been vetted and are likely to be looking for a similar relationship. Matchmakers will save your child energy and time so they can concentrate on other activities, work, and personal relationships.

Ask friends and other family members to fix them up

Last on the list of top dating strategies is the blind date. Sure, blind dates aren't always successful. They can be nerve-wracking because both people are walking into a meeting, well, blind. And your child may cringe at the suggestion. But a successful blind date can be an excellent way for your child to meet someone who is compatible. As you remember from the beginning of this chapter, I met my husband on a blind date. Yes, I definitely have stories about blind dates that didn't work: the guy who wouldn't stop talking on his cell phone during dinner or the guy who took me to an "all you can eat buffet" and crammed food in his pockets, backpack, and coat. But it's a myth that blind dates don't work. It's also a myth that blind dates are only for the desperate. A blind date is about being open-minded—and being open to suggestions. In fact, when the couples in my study are asked about how they met, one of the most common answers is, "We were fixed up."

Here's why blind dates work: psychologists know that the best choice of a love partner (see later in this chapter) is based on the "likes attract" rule. That is, people should seek a partner who shares their life values. I'll discuss this further on page 197, but it's **similarity in key life values** that keeps love relationships together over time. And surprisingly, although it may sound fun and exciting, it **isn't similarity in interests, hobbies, or even personality** that keep relationships happy and healthy over time. And who better to find someone similar to you than the people who love and care about you—your family and friends! In other words, the people who are fixing up your child with potential love matches typically select others they think are similar. They want what is generally best for your child! So, why not tune into their suggestions?

IS THIS RELATIONSHIP RIGHT FOR YOUR CHILD?

When your child starts dating someone, it's only natural for them to think about the future. How can they tell if they're in love? Is this something serious? Could this person be "the one"? Let's dive into how your child can discover that this is the right relationship for them, by discussing what I call "The Love Doctor's Two-Part Safety Check."

Checkpoint #1: Ask themselves about their feelings

To find out if the relationship has a future, they need to start with their feelings. There appear to be two distinct types of love that occur in romantic relationships: **a love of passion** that's the first-blush love when the relationship is young, and **a love filled with**

friendship that keeps relationships together and truly happy over the long term.

Passionate love is an intense emotion that has a physiological foundation. Your heart rate increases, you feel a rush of adrenaline go through your body, and a cascade of love chemicals floods your brain, (see box below).

At the beginning of a love relationship, your child will experience a high level of passionate love because everything is new and exciting. They'll be learning interesting and novel information about their love interest every day, and this fuels the passion. Most people become intoxicated at the beginning of a new love relationship. They'll be walking on air and everything in life will seem bigger, brighter, and better. They won't be able to get this person out of their mind, and they'll be filled with a desperate longing to be with their love interest.

DID YOU KNOW?

Those 24/7 thoughts and feelings that your child has about a new love interest are actually driven by biological chemicals. Levels of dopamine, norepinephrine, testosterone, phenylethylamine, and serotonin spike in the brain when we are experiencing romantic love. It's a potent cascade of love chemicals that influences our mood, how rational we are, and our romantic responses.

You've heard the phrase "love is blind." Well, at the beginning of a new relationship, it's true! As your child is experiencing passionate love, they will idealize their love partner and see them through "rose-colored glasses." In fact, studies show while in the throes of passionate love, people actually ignore or minimize their partner's faults or any information that isn't flattering.

Rather than seeing the real person, flaws and all, they will see the other person for who they need or want them to be. He isn't kind to your parents? Your child doesn't even notice. She's always late or doesn't help clear the table? That is no big deal.

But as time goes by and the passionate love (or infatuation) wears off, your child will take those rose-colored glasses off and they will see the imperfections that every partner and every person has. They will begin to really know and see that love partner for who they really are. In fact, science[29] shows that it can take as long as 12–18 months of being together before the brain's love chemicals stabilize. This is an inevitable, natural part of any relationship. Psychologist Ted Huston[30] followed couples over time and found that after only 18–24 months of being with someone, passionate love **decreased to 50%** of what it was at the beginning of the relationship!

As passionate love declines, the second type of love, called **companionate love,** actually increases (and if it doesn't, it might not be the right relationship). Companionate love is the love that's characterized by support, friendship, and commitment. It also has a physiological foundation. Your body starts producing oxytocin, which is the hormone that triggers relaxation and promotes emotional bonding.

When I talk to couples who have been together for 15 years or more, most of them attribute their happiness to the friendship and support of their partner. Without fail, they report being great friends and companions. The feeling of knowing another person so well and fitting so comfortably together, like a glove on a hand, is really what makes companionate love such a powerful and profound force. And although passion and romance are vital to a long-lasting relationship, they are not the glue that holds a relationship together over the long haul.

That's why your child should take their time when dating. And before they decide if a relationship is right for them, they want to ask themselves about their personal feelings or about their love experience with the partner. As a parent, I'm sure you remember at least one love experience where the person you thought you were in love with turned out to be *someone else entirely.* Maybe your sweet and friendly girlfriend turned out to be a sweet and too-friendly flirt. Or the guy who wanted to spend all of his time with you wasn't incredibly loving; he was just jealous and insecure. Or, maybe those little things that were once so endearing became very unattractive over time. When you think about some of your past relationships, do you groan and mumble, "What was I thinking?" Well, for you (and for your child), the cascade of biological love chemicals can work for you.

This may be worrisome to you as a parent. You're likely thinking, *Is* **passionate love the right state of mind** *for my child to make sound decisions about a partner?* Is it even possible for them to see who someone is, inside and out, after so little time? *Probably not.* For that, they need to take their time, even up to a year with the same partner, to see if companionate love has developed!

Relationship Advice in Action

"My daughter moved in with her boyfriend after four months together. She didn't see his faults and thought he was the best thing. But they weren't compatible. It didn't last long because she saw that she made the decision too quickly, before she really got to know him. Now she and I have talked about the differences between lust and love, and the importance of waiting until you can see the person for who they really are."
—*relationship survey response*

That's why it's vital to share this science-based information with your child. Disclose some of your own personal memories, of when the person you thought you were in love with turned out to be someone else entirely. Talk about passionate love, being in the throes of passion, and how love is blind—preferably *before* they get into a relationship! But even if your child is already in a new relationship, it's never too late to discuss the science and biology behind passionate and companionate love. Encourage them to not make any big decisions in the throes of passion, such as living together or getting married.

How to distinguish love from lust

There are many complexities to love and each person may experience it in a unique way. But what are the differences between love and lust?

When your child is drawn to someone based *solely* on passion or sexual desire, it may feel like love to them, but in reality, it's actually lust—and lust is yet another feeling that's directly influenced by the body's hormones. The hormone testosterone directly contributes to feelings of lust: the higher the level of active testosterone in a person's bloodstream, the more sexual desire a person experiences, and the more often they have sexual thoughts.

Can this be confused or misinterpreted as romantic love? Absolutely!

Now, your child *can* have both in a relationship—they can lust after *and* love their partner. But there are four specific clues to help your child distinguish lust from love:

1. **They want their partner to connect with their family.**
   When your child is in love, they are happy when their love partner connects with other people in their life and gets along with the people who are important to them. Also,

they want their love partner to get a sense of their past, and they like the idea that their family and friends are impressed by this person.

2. **They speak in "we," not "I."** When two people are in love, their lives are intertwined. By habit, they think of themselves as a "we" or an "us" rather than a "me," "him," or "her." For example, when people ask your child what they did this past weekend, they might automatically respond by saying, "We went to the movies and had a fantastic dinner," rather than, "I went to the movies, and I went to dinner afterwards."

3. **They want to share information.** Love prompts your child to share extensive personal, and often confidential, information with their partner. They feel an urge to share things about their childhood, desires, feelings, and aspirations for the future. By looking at the topics and the content of the information they're discussing with their love partner, they will understand whether they're in lust or love.

4. **They influence each other.** When two people love each other, what one partner does or wants to do influences the other in strong and meaningful ways. For example, if your child wanted to move to another city for work, or was contemplating a big change, their love partner would be involved in that decision. Similarly, love would mean that in a medical scare or work termination they would turn to their partner for support.

QUIZ: Is It Just Infatuation?

Lust, also known as infatuation, can feel like an obsession. During this period, your child may feel like a relationship superhero with powers of ultra-focused attention, heightened energy, no need for food or sleep, feelings of euphoria, and unstoppable sexual energy and attraction. They may swear that what they're feeling is love, but they may actually be a victim of their body's hormones instead. Studies[31] have found that the average person experiences infatuation at least four or five times over their lifetime. Here are several questions to ask:

1. Is their relationship distracting them from work or other responsibilities?

2. Are they having a hard time concentrating and staying focused on anything other than their new partner?

3. Do they constantly feel the need to be together, even if they have to sneak away from other responsibilities?

4. Are they ditching activities they used to enjoy (or are they neglecting their friends and family) to spend time with their new love instead?

5. Do they ignore or not care what their friends or family think about the relationship?

6. Have they recently lost weight or find that they just aren't hungry?

7. Do they constantly think about their future with the partner, and what their partner thinks about them?

They should give themselves one point for each "yes" response, then tally their score. The higher the number, the more likely it is that they are infatuated with their partner, at least for now. My advice? If they have a high score, they should slow down and take their time in the relationship. They're probably not seeing their partner and the relationship clearly. Don't make any big decisions about their relationship right now.

Checkpoint #2: Ask themselves about the relationship

Now that your child has assessed their feelings, it's time to evaluate the relationship itself. Are there any "signs" that will reveal whether your child and their love partner are *truly* compatible? Yes, there are. There are three crucial questions your child should ask themselves. Their answers will help them determine if that relationship is right for them.

QUESTION #1: DO THEY TRUST EACH OTHER?

As discussed in Chapter 1, trust is the most important and essential aspect of any relationship. When you trust someone, you believe that person tells you the truth, won't hurt or deceive you, and has your best interests at heart. In a loving relationship, this faith and trust reduces your inhibitions and worries, which allows you and your partner to share feelings and dreams with each other, and to feel closer and more connected.

Before your child makes a commitment or takes a next step in their relationship, they should ask themselves: *Am I able to trust my love partner?* In order to answer that, they can have what I call a "trust chat," where they ask their partner tough questions, like "What do trust and commitment mean to you?" and "Is it acceptable to keep secrets from one another? If so, what kinds of secrets are okay?" This conversation will give them a sense of how much they trust each other, and whether they view trust the same way. It takes courage and confidence to initiate an honest and intimate conversation like this with a partner. But it's far better to understand in advance what makes their relationship work well, rather than being confronted later with the challenge of figuring out why things fell apart.

Of course, trust is also about *their partner's* trustworthiness. But how can your child know if their partner is the kind of person who can be trusted? While there are no guarantees, there are five cues that may point to the fact that they are. Share these signals with your child. Ideally, discuss these signals before they get into a relationship (or when you have a trust chat with your child, see Chapter 1 page 23), but even if your child is already in a new relationship, it's never too late to discuss.

1. **Is their partner consistent and predictable?** Does your child's love partner behave the same way each time they are stressed out, upset, or full of love? If a person's reactions are consistent, you can usually predict their behavior in the future. Consistent behavior is a key to trustworthiness.

2. **Does their partner have a good relationship history?** If your child's partner valued their past relationship(s) and had an amicable split, that's a good sign. On the other hand, if their partner's relationship history is a sordid tale of flings and bitter exes, it's tempting for your child to think that they're the one person fabulous enough to turn things around. But that is not likely to happen. People tend to repeat patterns unless they are consciously motivated to change.

3. **Is their partner dependable and reliable?** When their partner says they are going to do something, do they come through most of the time? Are they reliable? Could your

child depend on the partner if they were sick and needed to be taken to the doctor, for example?

4. **Has their partner been honest with them so far?** It's fine to protect people from some information (a little privacy isn't a bad thing), but if they hide *important* information (e.g., financial assets and debts; see Chapter 6, page 173), your child and their partner can't grow as a couple. If their partner regularly lies, fabricates information, or makes statements that contradict the truth, it will eat away at the relationship.

5. **Does their partner have their best interests at heart?** Does their partner think of your child, and what might be best for them, when making decisions separately *and* as a couple? This includes what they do as a couple, where they go on dates, and how they support each other's friendships, career, and life decisions.

AT A GLANCE: When Jealousy Rears Its Ugly Head

Jealousy is among the most human of all emotions, and it has the power to bring out the worst in us, especially when we're in a relationship. Jealousy happens when you think you're going to lose a relationship with a person you really value. However, unlike trust, jealousy is typically a *one-way street*: when you are jealous, it involves *your* emotions, and your emotions alone. Sometimes, jealousy is warranted. But often, it is not.

Jealousy comes in two common forms: *reactive jealousy* and *suspicious jealousy*—and the distinction between the two is very important.

Reactive jealousy occurs when a person becomes aware of an actual threat or danger to the relationship. For example, when a person finds out that their partner has been unfaithful or has made romantic or sexual plans with someone else, reactive jealousy is almost always the result, and rightfully so.

Suspicious jealousy, on the other hand, comes up when your partner *hasn't* misbehaved. Your suspicions don't match up with the facts at hand, and there isn't any proof that your partner has engaged in a behavior that would threaten your relationship. Let's say you are seated at a bar and notice that an attractive stranger is smiling at your partner. A victim of suspicious jealousy might see this as a threat: you might feel sick to your stomach or get angry at your partner for flirting with the stranger. Taken to its extreme (as it so often is in books, movies, and on TV shows), this type of jealousy is typically followed by a swift punch in the nose, a drink in someone's face, or a heated argument.

Even if your child is *convinced* that their partner is up to something—maybe something doesn't feel right, or they have a bad feeling in their gut—but they can't prove it, they are still dealing with suspicious jealousy. Their gut could very well be right. But it could also be wrong. The truth is, they may never know—and their suspicious jealousy could very well destroy their relationship.

If your child finds themselves succumbing to an attack of "the green-eyed jealous monster," use these tips to help them face the issue:

- **Look inside.** Are they making something out of nothing? Are they dependent on their relationship and how it makes them feel about themselves? The more they depend on their partner for feelings of self-worth, the more likely it is that they'll be fighting the green-eyed monster. Focus on gaining some independence from the relationship: spend time with family or friends who think they're great or immerse themselves in learning something new that will build their confidence.

- **Be honest and listen carefully.** Even if there's no good reason to be jealous, it's time for a heart-to-heart conversation. They should discuss the issue *directly* and listen carefully to their partner's response. Does your child's partner care about their worries or concerns? If their partner is blatantly misbehaving—for example, by flirting to get attention right in front of them—your child needs to be clear about how these behaviors make them feel. For example, "I'm not sure why you are paying so much attention to my co-worker, but it is making me feel insecure and uncomfortable."

- **Ask for help.** Some insecurities can be easily cured when they are "cosmetic" in nature. (For example, your child might find that they feel more confident with themselves—and less prone to suspicious jealousy—after losing a few pounds or buying new clothes.) However, some expressions of jealousy, including inappropriate behaviors like stalking or calling at all hours of the day and night, may be a sign of deeper-seated insecurities that are best resolved with the help of a professional.

QUESTION #2: DO THEY SHARE SIMILAR LIFE VALUES?

The next question your child wants to ask themselves before they decide that this relationship is right for them is whether the two of them share similar **key life values**. Key life values are the parts of life that are most important to your child. They are the underlying attitudes and beliefs that make them the person they are.

Many people are attracted to their opposite. But the EYM study and others[32] show that when love partners share similar values and beliefs, they experience greater relationship happiness over time. Shared values are important because they act as a frame of reference and enhance a couple's communication by creating a kind of emotional shorthand. Sharing a similar perspective or set of experiences—like views on money, religion, or how you raise children—makes it easier for couples to see each other's points of view and understand each other's feelings. If your child and their partner aren't compatible on life values, they may want to think carefully about whether this is the right relationship for them. If your child is open to it, share the below quiz with them. Perhaps take the quiz with your child first, as a bonding moment and to talk through the choices. Then encourage them to do the quiz with their love partner.

QUIZ: The Love Doctor's Compatibility Checklist

Are you and your partner truly compatible? Do you share the same life values? If the two of you haven't talked about this yet, use this quiz to kick-start your conversation.

In the first column, check the **three statements** you feel are most important to you. In the second column, do the same for your partner, checking off the **three statements** you feel are most important to them. Then, have your partner answer on their own (checking off what's most important to them, and what's most important to you)—and match your answers up.

(continued)

YOU PARTNER

☐ ☐ Saving money for my future takes priority over everyday spending.

☐ ☐ I believe in enjoying life and spending money when I need to.

☐ ☐ Having children and a family are an important part of my future.

☐ ☐ A family unit is stronger when one parent can stay at home.

☐ ☐ Religion and faith are part of my everyday life.

☐ ☐ I'm open-minded and don't have issues with an interfaith partnership.

☐ ☐ I don't believe in organized religion.

☐ ☐ I derive satisfaction from excelling in my career, and I don't mind putting in the hours to make this happen.

☐ ☐ I believe in finding a healthy balance between work and my personal life.

☐ ☐ Life is for living. I wouldn't work if I didn't have to.

☐ ☐ I take care of myself, work out, and make healthy food choices.

☐ ☐ I don't have time for exercise and cooking, and usually eat out.

Do your partner's answers and key life values match up with your own? Do you know each other well? Does your partner feel the same way about money, children, spirituality, careers, or personal health? Couples don't have to share *all* life values, but sharing each other's most important key life values is vital for a healthy long-term love.

QUESTION #3: HOW DO THEY HANDLE CONFLICT?

The last relationship question for your child is: "How do my partner and I manage our disagreements?" They should stop for a moment and think about the last difference, argument, or disagreement they had with their partner. Did they interrupt one another or call each other names, raise their voice or cry, say things they regretted afterwards? Did their partner? Or were they able to listen to their partner's perspective and remain respectful of their opinions?

As you've learned in Chapter 5, conflict is a natural part of any relationship. All couples are bound to have differences and disagreements. The key to "healthy conflict" is in how you treat each other when you're at odds. And, how your child and their love partner behave now when they have a disagreement says a lot about how they will (or won't) resolve problems in the future. In my study, how couples managed their conflict and disagreements was a key predictor in whether they stayed together over time.

If couples handle disagreements in a destructive way—with cursing, screaming, or talking down to their partner—my research shows that they are *more than twice as likely* to break up over time. A good relationship is one where the two partners fight fair. It's important to pick your battles, know when to engage in an argument (and know when to let it go), skip the name-calling, and calm down when you talk. These are similar strategies for how to manage conflict that we discussed in Chapter 5. Sit down with your child and discuss how they handle disagreements and differences with their partner— whether it be big differences (e.g., religious differences over the holidays, how to spend money) or small ones (e.g., where should we go for dinner, does your friend come with us to the store). Partners who have more level-headed conversations than screaming matches and door-slamming fights are more compatible in the long run.

RELATIONSHIPS AND SEX

Families have different values and approaches to the topic of sex in relationships, so these discussions may not be easy—try to be patient; respect differences between you and your young adult child; don't take resistance personally and come back to the discussions at a later age or point in time if you're met with defensiveness; continue to build trust, self-disclose, and give affirmations to your child; and remember to ask the right kinds of questions in the conversations (see Chapter 2). Ideally, the topic of relationships and sex is a conversation you would have *before* your child gets into a relationship. But even if your child is already in a new relationship, it's never too late to discuss the role that sex plays in their love relationships.

The key thing to remember to share in these conversations about sex and relationships is that *when* they decide to have sex with a love partner is *their* decision. If they don't feel good about a situation or the timing, they should wait until they do. They should be honest with themselves and their partner, and not let anyone pressure them. In therapy, I ask many clients, "What is your *motivation* for wanting to become sexually active with a new partner? Do you want to show someone that you love them? Is it for physical pleasure?" You can share these questions with your young adult child and encourage them to identify their motivation for having sex with a new partner, even if they don't share that information with you.

Sharing their reasons for wanting sex with a partner *with you* is not the goal of these questions. Instead, the goal is to help them understand the motivation behind their desired actions and to feel okay about that reason. Also, being physically intimate with someone can bring out a whole new set of fears and concerns. Tell your child that **you're always there for them** if they want to discuss anything with you. This support is vital, regardless of whether you agree or disagree with their reason or decision. Sex is about timing, emotion, and safety. Here are four things to consider when they "start thinking about sex" in a relationship:

1. **There is great diversity in when sex comes into a relationship.** According to a Child Trends report,[33] which used a study of 14,322 U.S. students between 18 and 25 years old, there is great diversity in terms of the length of time that young adults knew their partner before having sex with them. "Thirty-one percent of young adults reported that they engaged in sex with their partner within the first month of knowing them. Thirty percent waited one to five months before having sex, fourteen percent waited six to eleven months, and twenty-five percent waited a full year or more. Only five percent knew their partner only one day prior to having sex."

2. **Waiting means safer and better sex.** Research[34] shows that waiting to have sex until you truly know your partner results in better and safer sex. If you wait, (a) sex is more likely to be planned, (b) sex is more likely to be talked about, and (c) sex is more likely to be protected or involve contraception.

3. **Most young adults use some form of contraception.** According to the same Child Trends report, two-thirds of young adults (68%) reported using some method of contraception the last time they had sex, including 34% who used condoms.

4. **Talk about sex before you have sex.** There's a myth that if you plan ahead, talk about sex, and ask your partner if they want to have sex, that sex won't be as exciting or enjoyable. The truth? The same research in #2 shows the

opposite. Communication about sex actually *increases* sexual satisfaction. People who talk candidly about sex with their partners (e.g., sexual histories, medications, needs, desires, concerns) have more fulfilling sexual encounters than those who don't. Talking about sex is challenging for many people however, because they don't have the vocabulary to comfortably speak about their sexuality. Here are a few questions they can ask:

- Are you comfortable introducing sex into our relationship?

- What are you comfortable with? Is anything off limits?

- Have you been tested for STIs (sexually transmitted infections)? And if so, when?

- Are you comfortable using condoms?

- How sexual have you been in your previous relationships?

- What do you like to do sexually? What have you done sexually in previous relationships?

REVIEWING THE STRATEGIES: MAKE A BIG DEAL ABOUT THE RIGHT RELATIONSHIP

When your child is in the right love relationship, the whole world seems brighter. There are **four top ways for them to meet potential love interests**. To determine if a relationship is right for them, use **"The Love Doctor's Two-Part Safety Check"**: (1) identify if it's really love or just infatuation/lust, and (2) ask themselves if they trust their partner, share life values, and manage conflict/differences in a healthy way. At the beginning of a relationship, **the body's biological chemicals take over**, causing people to overlook their partner's faults. Studies show that it can take 12 to 18 months before people are able to see their love partner **for who they really are**. This inevitable decline in passionate love is a natural part of the process of relationships as they develop over time.

While infatuation and lust are exciting, **companionate love**—a love built on support, intimacy, and friendship—is what keeps couples together over time. You can help your child ask three questions to see if a relationship is right for them.

Strategies recap

Top Four Ways to Find Potential Love Partners

- Join an activity that meets regularly

- Join an online dating app

- Hire a matchmaker

- Get fixed up

Understanding the Experience of Love

- Understand passionate love and companionate love

- Distinguish love from lust/infatuation

- Involving your partner with your family/friends, thinking in "we" versus "I," revealing and sharing highly personal information, and making big decisions together are all signs of companionate love.

Is a Relationship Right for Your Child?

- Do they trust their partner?

- Are their key life values a match?

- Do they fight fair?

Talking about Sex

- Regardless of family values, be open and patient when speaking to your child about sex.

- Stress that they need to do what's right for them.

- Tell them you're always there for them, regardless of what they choose.

- They should talk about sex with their partner before having sex.

CHAPTER 8

Handle Heartbreaks and Other Love Challenges

My daughter had been dating a man for over a year. They met at a conference that she attended while in graduate school and they continued to connect afterwards. He cared about her and she meant the world to him. She and I had many talks about their relationship and things seemed good between the two of them. We had him over our house many times, for family meals, holidays, celebrations, and outdoor fun. He even came with us to a family reunion over the summer for five days. My entire extended family liked him and felt comfortable with him, which is not a given, because we are all introspective and question-oriented. As I spent more time with him, I became attached. My husband and I even spent time with his family, when they came from out of town to visit one weekend. His mother and I totally clicked.

Last week, my daughter came home for dinner. We sat at the kitchen table, and she explained that she was breaking up with this man. She had her reasons but was nonetheless quite upset and sad. My first reaction was to help her cope with the heartbreak she was experiencing. We talked for hours. We discussed how she felt and what she was going to tell him. After she left, I began to realize that I was sad and disappointed that I wouldn't see him or his mother ever again! I had become invested in their relationship. Should I have become attached to him? I struggled with the notion of whether it was better for me to have remained at a distance for a longer period. I was bewildered about what I should do in the future with my children's partners.

This is just one of many "love challenges" that you will face as your adult child experiences the world of dating, relationships, and love. You may struggle with what to do and say, or how to act and feel. *That's why you're reading this book!* And you are not alone.

I've talked to hundreds of parents who have experienced similar love struggles and challenges with their young adult children. We don't always know how to manage these situations. And I can't say it strongly enough: **The key message is that there are high stakes in how you handle these love challenges**. Your reactions and what you say when your adult child experiences these struggles can have repercussions for your child's love relationships *and* your long-term relationships with your child.

The previous seven chapters in this book all addressed how to discuss or introduce specific relationship processes (or to model in your own relationship) to help your child have happy, healthy relationships. In this chapter, I take a different approach. I discuss the most common love challenges that you might face with your young adult child. You'll learn what the love challenges are and why they are difficult. I'll provide you with specific ways to address or deal with these love challenges that will preserve your healthy, happy relationship with your child over the long haul *and* improve your child's love relationships.

This chapter also will be organized a bit differently from the other chapters in this book. I'll present a specific love challenge story and then strategies and tips to handle that situation. The stories come from clients, students, friends, or parents in my workshops and research studies (with all identifying information removed). Before I move on to the most common love challenges, I want to share **two overall tips** that apply to *all* of the love challenges that you might experience with your young adult child.

First, you learned in Chapter 5 (page 148) that when you disagree or have conflict with your love partner, it is essential to **stay calm**. Solving problems when you are upset is nearly impossible. The brain needs at least 30 minutes to return to normal functioning. After you calm down, you are much more likely to see things in a new light. The same strategy holds true if you feel yourself getting upset with your child.

I recognize that staying calm isn't always easy to practice. When you are emotional, it can be very hard to be composed. But it is vital that you try to stay calm. Think about this five-step process when you experience a love challenge with your child:

1. Focus on your breathing, in and out.

2. Count to 10—slowly.

3. Remind yourself: "My struggle doesn't say anything about me as a parent."

4. Think about the advice I shared in this chapter for the specific challenge you're experiencing.

5. Practice what you've learned in this chapter.

Second, it is important to remind your child that **you are there for them**. I mention this in Chapter 7 as well. This support for them is *vital*, no matter what love challenge they are facing, and regardless of whether you agree or disagree with their love decisions or how you feel about their partner. Make clear that you are available to help them should they want your assistance. They may not take your advice right away, but they need to know that you're there if they need you.

> ### Relationship Advice in Action
>
> "One fundamental thing that I have stressed with all of my children is that I am there for them, no matter what! I even tell them that I don't have to agree with their relationship decision. I just don't want them to need assistance or be in trouble and not think of reaching out to me." —*relationship survey response*

TOP COMMON LOVE CHALLENGES

Let's look at the most common love challenges that you might experience with your child. Many of these challenges will sound familiar. I will share simple strategies to effectively cope with each one.

Love Challenge #1: Your Child Experiences Heartbreak

It's impossible for your child to go through life without disappointment, hurt, and relationship breakups. Heartbreaks are extremely hard, both for the person who's initiating the breakup and for the person on the receiving end, no matter how long the relationship lasted. There will be grief, anger, and sadness. When two people really care about each other, it will hurt when the relationship ends—even if you didn't think the relationship was serious, you wondered if your child was invested or attached, or you're happy that the relationship is over.

Granted, a positive breakup can be challenging, but your goal is to help your child keep their sense of worth, learn from the relationship, and eventually move on. For example, in one of our sessions, my client Esther talked about her daughter's heartbreak, vividly recalling Aurora's late-night phone call that woke her up from a sound sleep with a jolt. Aurora was sobbing and said that her boyfriend had broken up with her only three days before their three-year anniversary. Esther comforted her daughter as best as she could and asked her if she wanted to come over in the morning. When Aurora arrived for breakfast, Esther found herself unable to find the right words, and fumbled through an awkward pep-talk that only made Aurora's frown deepen.

When Esther brought this up with me, we discussed the following strategies to help her navigate Aurora's heartbreak:

1. **Don't press too hard.** This can be a difficult topic for your child to confess or discuss with you. So just being available and supportive is the first step. Be empathic.

2. **Listen and ask questions.** Give your child the space and time to tell you what happened. And then listen well (see Chapter 4). Sometimes we want to tell our child what to do or how to feel. Don't dismiss how they are feeling. Don't lecture them when they're feeling hurt. Listen and ask questions that respond to what they are telling you. Talking through how and why the relationship ended will allow your child to make sense of what's happened and give meaning to it, which will help them feel better and move on.

3. **Schedule time together.** If you think your child is having a really hard time with the breakup, schedule several times to get together. They don't need to talk about the breakup with you every time, but they may need your company.

4. **Give the type of help that's needed.** The type of support you give should match the type of support your child wants to receive; otherwise, it is not supportive or very

helpful. There are two types of support: *emotional support* is when your child needs sympathy, affection, acceptance, and reassurance; *problem-focused support* is in the form of information and guidance. Do they need a shoulder to cry on and a sympathetic ear? Or do they need concrete advice and practical solutions? I always tell my clients and workshop participants that it is okay to ask: "Are you looking for some practical advice, or would you prefer that I just listen?" Asking your child which type of support they want is an act of real sensitivity and caring.

5. **Encourage special strengths.** Every child has a gift or unique strength. After a breakup, your child may not feel great about themselves because rejection can be difficult. Remind your child what is really special about them, like being a good singer, writer, athlete, student, hard worker, or friend.

6. **Help manage anger/sadness/frustration.** A breakup can be very traumatic and if your child is looking for ways to cope and constructively reduce the hurt and pain, you can suggest several healthy outlets for their emotions, such as keeping a journal; meditating; exercising outside or at the gym; talking to a mentor, older sibling, or friend; or expressing themselves in their favorite creative way. Volunteering in their community is a great way for them to become less concerned with their own struggles by putting the focus on others. They could write a letter to their ex-partner, to get their feelings out—*but they should not send the letter.* This exercise is for them only, not to win back their former partner.

7. **Tune into red flags.** Look for any signals that indicate your child is having major problems. Look for major changes in behavior over a period of time, like big changes in their work habits, how they dress or in their personal hygiene, in their eating or sleeping habits, or withdrawal from friends or other extracurricular activities. If things get really tough, suggest they seek professional help with a counselor, therapist, teacher, social worker, psychologist, or religious advisor.

SIMPLE TIPS: Five Dos and Don'ts

Five things to say to soothe the broken-hearted:

1. I understand how you're feeling.

2. I have felt this way before and I can only imagine how hurt you are.

3. I'm here for you when you need me.

4. Let's figure out what we can do about this together.

5. How can I help you?

Five things *not* to say:

1. I never liked your partner anyway.

2. You can't really feel that bad; you were only together a short time.

3. Don't worry, you'll find someone else.

4. Why did you break up with them? They were the best.

5. It's been a long time already; aren't you ready to stop feeling sorry for yourself?

Love Challenge #2: Your Child is in an Unhealthy Relationship, and They Come to Get Your Advice

Most people don't listen to their gut feelings about the red flags or unhealthy habits in their love relationships. Your child is no exception—and they may be in relationships that are not good for them. I don't mean an abusive relationship. Rather, it just doesn't seem positive *most* of the time and they're holding out, hoping the relationship will get better. Your child may come to you for advice and support, but you're not sure how to help them identify the unhealthy habits. For example, my client José was very happy that his son, who was 27 years old, came to him to seek his advice. His son was in a relationship of 18 months, and he was wondering if he should stay or leave the relationship. His son said that the first year of the relationship was pretty good. But for the last several months, it just seemed bad most of the time. His son didn't feel that he could turn to his partner for support, and he and his partner fought all the time. José and I talked about sharing with his son, the four signals (see below) that a love relationship is unhealthy.

If your child comes to you for advice, share with them the signals of an unhealthy love relationship. Ask them open-ended questions (see Chapter 2, page 69) to help them identify whether their relationship is unhealthy. Here are four signs to share with your child that their relationship may be unhealthy. One or two of these signs on their own may not mean they should leave their relationship. Instead, it indicates that a relationship has serious issues that need attention.

1. **There's conflict and anger.** The first signal of an unhealthy relationship is that the relationship or home life with this person is generally cold, angry, and conflicted. If your child or their partner consistently says mean or cruel

things about each other in front of you, other family, or friends, this is a sign of an unhealthy relationship.

2. **Partner support is lacking.** Another way of identifying an unhealthy relationship is when your child doesn't turn to their partner for assistance in stressful situations because their partner isn't there for them. Ask your child to think about the last time they experienced stress about a job, a health scare, or an issue with a friend. Did they think about turning to their partner for emotional support? An unhealthy relationship is one where they would prefer to get help from anyone *but* their partner.

3. **Their partner is avoiding them.** Sometimes people have to work late or have many commitments that don't include their love partner. But another sign of an unhealthy relationship is if the partner *chooses* to work late or *increases* their obligations because they don't want to be with their significant other.

4. **Can't say "I love you" anymore.** Every relationship has its ups and downs, and no relationship is perfect. There will be times when your child may not like what their partner has done or said. They may not even want to say "I love you" to the partner loud and clear. But an unhealthy relationship is one where they can't say the words to their partner anymore at all.

Challenge #3: The Partner isn't Right for Your Child

Sometimes you aren't thrilled with your child's love partners. **It's not that your child is in an unhealthy relationship,** but instead, **you think that this partner isn't the best for your child or you believe**

they could do better. This may be because of a specific characteristic, such as already having children, not working hard enough or being motivated, having no long-term goals, not being respectful, or not wanting to get married. Perhaps you think they are incompatible with your child because of different religious beliefs or unequal job potential/earnings. When you are worried about your child's short- or long-term investment in this love relationship, how do you discuss these concerns without making them defensive or causing withdrawal from any future discussions? Can you get them to consider incompatibilities without starting a disagreement?

One of my clients, Karen, and her wife Charlotte, have dealt with their daughter's boyfriend for almost two years now. Liam claims to love their daughter, Olivia, and she loves him back. But accepting Liam has always been difficult for Karen and Charlotte. Having Liam at the dining room table tends to lead to a night that is irritating at best, yet Olivia always smiles when he is around, and continues to ask Karen and Charlotte to give him a break. They just can't seem to shake their distaste for him. Karen came to me for help with her relationship with Olivia and for advice on how to manage this situation.

I had a story to share with Karen, one that involves my own parents, from whom I learned some effective tips. When I was 25 years old, I was working very hard at getting my PhD, interning at the University of Wisconsin Counseling Center, conducting research, and teaching undergraduate students. I barely had time for myself. I was in a relationship with a man who wasn't the right person for me. He was spontaneous, passionate about social causes, and very personable—all qualities that I found extremely attractive at that time. Yet, he was emotionally unstable, unmotivated to get a job, lacked any long-term goals, stayed out late, had no money, and didn't want children or to get married. I was blinded by the relationship and the emotions I thought I felt at the time. My parents were rightly concerned, and I often wondered how they kept themselves composed and calm. They never said he wasn't right for me. They never told me to stop dating him. They never said they didn't like him. In fact, I'm not sure what would have happened had they judged me and stated their opinion.

Instead, my father and mother—separately—would open conversations by asking me what I liked about this man, and how he made me happy. I never felt attacked or defensive. Inevitably, these questions would generate answers that I think my parents wanted me to see: **the two of us were not compatible**. Their open-ended questions led me down a path where *I came up with what I thought at the time was an epiphany*—he was not the right person for me! Oh, my parents were so smart!

Here are the four strategies that I learned from my parents—and later shared with Karen:

1. **Don't judge.** Don't criticize your child's partner. Do not volunteer that you think that the partner isn't right for them. Even if they ask, **tread lightly and cautiously**. Lecturing your child about someone they've chosen as a love partner can lead to defensiveness and pushing them toward, rather than away from, that partner.

2. **Work as a team.** Instead of letting your child know that you don't think the current partner is the best (or that they could do better), try to lead them to discover that on their own. When you work together as a team—to help them analyze the situation (see #3 below) and come up with answers themselves (e.g., "this partner is not right for me")—they are significantly more likely to act on that belief.

3. **Ask probing questions.** Ask (a) How does this partner make you happy? (b) Can you see yourself with this person in three or five years from now? (c) Do you think the two of you trust each other? (d) Have the two of you talked about commitment and trust? (e) How do the two of you handle conflict and stress together? and (f) Do you and your partner have similar key life values? These are topics I presented as key relationship processes that keep relationships strong and healthy over time (see Chapter 7, page 192). In addition, ask about the differences between your child and their partner. For example, if your child wants a family, how does the partner feel about having a family?

4. **Learn to say when.** Many parents bang their heads against a wall trying—often without success—to get their child to hear and understand that a partner isn't right for them. At some point, you need to accept the fact that your child is a young adult and must discover things on their own. Don't take this personally. You simply have to learn to be decent and get along with the partner, particularly if you want to continue to be a part of your child's life.

Relationship Advice in Action

"One of the things I've definitely learned (the hard way) with my children is that *'everything'* I say to them about their partners and whether I get along with their partners is key to their relationship happiness (and my well-being). I've decided not to be critical nor judge the partners anymore. Instead, I'll ask my children for their perspectives and go from there." —*relationship survey response*

Love Challenge #4: Meeting Your Child's Partner for the First Time (Over the Holidays, No Less!)

Given the COVID-19 pandemic, it's possible that your child has been dating someone for almost two years who you have never met in person. Now, your child wants to bring their partner home for the holidays (or another time) to spend time with you. For example, William, who is a friend, mentioned that he was elated when his son, Ben, said he and his girlfriend would finally be able to visit. Ben had told William many stories about their time together in the past year, but William still felt like he had no clue who he was about to meet. He felt pressured to like this young woman, Ava, because he didn't want to upset his son.

Here are my tips for this situation, divided into three strategies to do ahead of time and three strategies to do as the gathering happens.

AHEAD OF TIME

1. **Set realistic expectations.** Setting realistic expectations is the key to not getting frustrated when your child's partner comes for the holidays. Accept that, in most situations, your relationship with the partner will develop slowly and your interactions may be awkward at first. The partner may not reveal much, or it may take many questions from you to open them up. Be patient and don't give up.

2. **Get to know them ahead of time.** Ask your child and their partner to video chat, Zoom, or FaceTime with you, before they head home for the holidays. Tell your child you miss them. Tell both of them how wonderful it is that they're coming for the holidays. Express how excited you are to meet the partner. Chat and get to know the partner. At the end of the call, ask your child's partner what their

favorite side dish or dessert is, and make sure to prepare it for the holiday gathering.

3. **Blend traditions.** Blending traditions ahead of time can help your child's partner feel at home with your family during the holidays. Ask your child to describe their partner's family rituals—such as special prayers, toasts, outdoor activities, or after-dinner games—and surprise your child and their partner with one of these favorite holiday rituals.

DURING THE HOLIDAY GATHERING

1. **Be inclusive.** When you make people feel valued, they are happier and more likely to return the affirmation. Do your best to help your child's partner feel that way. Giving compliments, asking open-ended questions, and being aware make people feel special. Show appreciation for the partner's manners or if they're helping you out.

2. **Respect differences.** Be a role model and respect everyone's opinion, particularly your child's partner. If there is a topic that creates too much conflict for you and your child/their partner, like politics and religion, try to stay clear of that topic.

3. **Keep it light.** Studies show that laughter and smiling change people's moods. The first time you meet your child's partner, particularly if it's over the holidays, you want to keep it light. Games and outdoor activities are always fun. Take out a board game to play with everyone or have each person come up with two things for which they are thankful in their lives to say during the holiday dinner.

Love Challenge #5: Your Child Decides to Visit their Partner's Family and Not You

Last week, one of my friends, Amelia, called to say that as she was finishing her holiday decorations around the house, she got this text from her son Noah: "Won't be home for the holidays. Going to see Lily's parents." She was taken aback by Noah's casual tone. While she understood his desire to see his partner's family, she felt hurt and abandoned. She was really looking forward to having Noah visit over the holidays.

Here are my tips for dealing with your disappointment and maintaining harmony between you and your child when they might not come home to visit when you had hoped they would:

1. **Don't take it personally.** Your child's decision is not about you. They didn't decide ***not*** to come home, but instead ***to go*** to their partner's family. It is actually a positive thing that your child recognizes that meeting their partner's family over the holidays is important. As long as your child has voluntarily made this decision, they are being a good partner and recognizing the needs of their significant other.

2. **Stay calm and respectful.** Be a good role model for your child and try to stay calm and composed. Breathe deeply to help yourself calm down. Take in some fresh air to soothe your emotions. Exercise, meditate, or do something creative. This will also demonstrate to your child that you can handle instances when things don't go as planned.

3. **Ask questions.** Instead of focusing on how disappointed you are, try to turn your focus on your child. Ask questions such as, "Are you comfortable going to your partner's

family?" "Do you have any concerns about going?" or "How are you feeling about going there for the holidays?" It might be emotionally challenging for them too. Tell your child that you will miss them and put a date on the calendar for when they (with or without their partner) can visit you.

4. **Affirm and check back.** Follow up a few days later with your child. Set aside time to make sure they are feeling comfortable with their decision. Assist them if they need anything for the visit. Suggest they bring something special to the holiday gathering for their partner's family. Make them feel good about their decision and tell them that you are proud of them, considering this was a difficult decision.

Love Challenge #6: Getting Attached to Your Child's Partner

At the beginning of this chapter, I shared with you the story of my daughter's breakup with her partner of one-and-a-half years and my recognizing that I had become invested in their relationship. I struggled with whether it was better for me to stay at a distance or continue to become attached to my children's love partners. At a workshop I gave a few years ago, one father stopped me and wanted to share his story. His name was Dan and he admitted that he was a bit overprotective when it came to his daughter, Sarah. Fittingly, Dan was suspicious of Sarah's partner Elise when they first met. Yet over the years, Dan formed a close bond with Elise. They enjoyed a similar interest in cooking, baking desserts, and watching cooking shows together. Dan started to view Elise as a great catch and was happy that Sarah found such a wonderful partner. Then one day Sarah came home crying and told her dad that Elise had decided to end the relationship. Her workplace was forcing her to move to a different state and she didn't want a long-distance relationship. Dan told me he was upset, not only because his daughter had had her heart broken, but because he felt he had lost a close friend.

Here are four points that I raised with Dan after he shared his story with me. I'm hoping to take some of my own advice, with my daughter now and with both of my children in the future.

1. **Are they actually a couple?** There is nothing wrong with being cautious and slow in getting attached to your child's love partners. Before you invite a new partner to meet you or the rest of the family, make sure that your child is on board, and they are a couple in the eyes of your child. You don't want to get involved when it's not necessary. Also, the level of your investment can depend on the stage of the relationship. You can get more attached and invested as the love relationship gets more serious and they reach a certain level of commitment.

2. **Set realistic expectations.** Try to accept that in most circumstances, the relationship between you and your child's partner will not be as close as that of the relationship between you and your child. Realistic expectations about how close, and what you can get from this relationship, is the best defense against developing hurt feelings.

3. **Connect with family.** When two people are in love, they want their partner to connect with the people who are important to them. They aspire to show this person off to others, and not just keep them to themselves. They want the partner to get a sense of their past, and they like the idea of having their family and friends spend time with and grow to

like this person. Remember, it's a good sign if you get along with your child's partner—for you and your child.

4. **Key connection for staying together.** In my EYM study, trying to get along with a partner's family was a common stressor. However, the statement, "My partner gets along with my family" (particularly when women said this) was a key predictor of who stayed together and who didn't. In the end, getting along with your child's partner matters for their relationship.

Challenge #7: Your Child and Partner Sleeping in the Same Room

Another love challenge you might experience is when your child, who is living out of town, comes home to visit with their partner. Is it okay for your child to share a room with their love partner in your house? For some parents, this is a non-issue. They recognize that their child is in a committed relationship and have no problem with offering them a single bedroom. In other circumstances, the child recognizes that the parent would feel uncomfortable and simply doesn't expect a shared room. In still other instances, this can be a delicate situation, where the parent struggles to balance their respect of their child as an autonomous young adult with the recognition of their own values and beliefs.

My client Jesse shared a situation that was relevant to this love challenge. He was filled with joy when his daughter asked if her partner, Brett, could join them for Thanksgiving this year. His daughter is in her senior year at college in a different state. Jesse and his wife like Brett and were looking forward to seeing both of them over the holiday. It didn't occur to Jesse to ask, until his wife was cleaning the extra bedroom downstairs, where his daughter and

Brett would sleep that weekend. Intuitively he was aware that his daughter might be sexually active, but that was very different from feeling comfortable knowing that they might be having sex in his house, while he was upstairs.

Here are three strategies that I discussed with Jesse about the upcoming visit:

1. **Identify your own beliefs/values.** Are you comfortable with your child sharing a room with their partner in your house? Be sure to understand where your beliefs come from. Also, are there conditions that might alter your beliefs? Have you met the partner before, is your child living with the partner, is their relationship longer-term rather than recent, will you be staying in your house vs. in a vacation house? Discuss your beliefs with your child's co-parent.

2. **Discuss with your child, ahead of time.** Start by telling your child that you are excited to visit with them and their partner. You can't wait to see them. You love them. Then, bring up the topic of sleeping arrangements in a non-threatening way ("What are your expectations regarding the sleeping arrangements?") or with "I" statements ("I would love to discuss where everyone will sleep in the house").

3. **Respect differences.** You and your child will not always see eye to eye. If this particular love challenge falls under one of those topics, you want to approach it like you would any difference of values. Validate your child's point of view. You don't have to agree with them, just acknowledge their thoughts and feelings ("I understand why you would want to sleep in the same room together"), and hopefully

they will follow your lead. This is not the time to lecture them about what is right and wrong, but instead, practice your good communication skills (see Chapter 4) and listen well. After all of the above, assuming that you haven't changed your viewpoint, you'll want to ask your child whether they can respect your values, while coming to visit you in your home, at least for this visit. Mention that you are open to discussing the topic for future visits. If they are not able to, then is some compromise possible, like staying at your sister's house or in a hotel?

Challenge #8: Age Differences Between Partners

As far as Hollywood is concerned, it is perfectly acceptable for two people to date when one is significantly older than the other. But you may struggle with understanding and accepting the relationship when there is a large age difference between your child and their partner. And what do you discuss with your child, if you're concerned about the obstacles down the road, if the relationship continues? My client Clark was unsure what to do when his daughter (age 24) told him that she was dating a man who had just turned 40. They had been dating for about five months before his daughter told him about her boyfriend and his age. Clark tried to hide his shocked expression. When he shared this situation and his feelings with me in our session, he said, "Dr. Orbuch, I have no idea what to do or say to my daughter! And can long-term relationships really work when there is such a significant age gap?"

Here are four strategies that Clark and I discussed:

1. **Consider emotional and psychological compatibility.**
   As children get older, it's not the chronological age that matters, but rather the emotional and psychological

compatibility between two people that is essential for a relationship. Rather than "do age differences really matter?" the better question is whether your child is compatible with their love partner in terms of beliefs, key life values, and goals.

2. **Discuss the future, not just the present.** Ask your child if they are considering this relationship long-term. Have they discussed whether they want children down the road, or is the older partner past that point in life? Other topics to discuss are retirement goals and career choices. For example, what if your child's older partner wants to retire soon and travel, yet your child wants to continue to work longer (or in Clark's daughter's case, start a career)?

3. **Set clear expectations.** You want your child to think about whether the age difference will affect the activities that they like to do with their partner, such as hiking, skiing, traveling, or even being able to take off from work. Have them share their general expectations for the relationship. Realistic expectations result in less frustration and disappointment.

4. **Important issues for everyone.** Let your child know that these conversations are topics *everyone* needs to consider when they enter a committed love relationship—not just when there are age differences.

Challenge #9: Navigating Online Dating and Relationships

While technology is making it easier for young adults to meet new partners, it has also created new challenges and risks. As discussed in Chapter 7, research shows that more than 40 million Americans turn to the internet or apps to find a love partner. Online dating is nothing new, but how do you help navigate and promote safe and healthy relationships for your child? For example, one of my students wanted to talk during my office hours about online dating. Carisa is a returning student (aged 55) and has sons who are 25 and 27 years old. She expressed concern about the fact that both of her sons were using dating apps and chatting regularly with women they were meeting online. She explained that she had met her current partner through a friend, so she wasn't totally sure what online dating safety tips to discuss with them, and what issues were essential for them to know as they meet people face-to-face after they met online.

Here are five topics that Carisa and I discussed about online dating and safety:

1. **Safety is key.** Safety is an important issue for all single people to consider, whether dating online or off. There's no reason to be apprehensive about meeting someone online, but discuss smart strategies with your child if they're dating online, particularly for the first few dates: (a) protect your identity and anonymity, (b) meet in populated and public locations, (c) meet the person at the location and drive yourself there and back, (d) don't drink too much or do anything that would impair your judgment, (e) don't leave your personal items unattended, and (f) tell a friend or family member about your plans.

2. **These dates can be successful.** Online dating is an extremely effective way to meet people. According to research,[35] 12% of Americans say they are married or in

a committed relationship with someone they first met through a dating site or app. Online dating opens up a much bigger and broader dating pool for your child, while still affording them total control. They choose the geographic scope for possible partners, whether it's across town or across the country, and they decide who might be right for them.

3. **Don't take rejections personally.** Your child may find that they send a lot of "hello" messages but receive few replies. Encourage them not to take a lack of response or a negative response personally. Help them shift their negative thoughts, *"no one ever likes me on this app,"* to positive experiences in their real life, like how they meet new friends very quickly and are well liked. The truth is that some people date online or with apps more for entertainment than to meet their soul mate.

4. **Take your time getting to know someone.** Studies show that relationships develop faster online, as we are more likely to reveal and respond to personal questions without the distractions of being with that person face-to-face. My advice is to wait at least one week, while continuing to chat online, before you meet face-to-face. Also, by being truthful from the start, your child will increase their odds of finding the right person.

5. **Be aware of lying or dishonesty.** There are several signals that your child can focus on to tell if someone isn't genuine or is lying to them. First, have your child pay attention to early warning signs and to listen to that gut feeling that something isn't right. For example, does

the potential suitor want to know all about your child but is silent about their own life? Or do they supply a phone number that is out of service or unable to accept messages? Second, your child should look for consistency in behaviors and answers to their questions. If someone is lying, they don't behave or answer in the same way each time a question is asked. For example, in one message they might talk about having a good job for the past two years, when in another chat they might say they just moved to the city and started a new job. Finally, if someone professes love or devotion too quickly, or within hours of meeting your child, it probably isn't true.

REVIEWING HOW TO HANDLE LOVE CHALLENGES

Whether your child has had their heart broken, you don't think their partner is compatible with them, or they are spending the holidays with their partner's family instead of yours, love challenges present situations where you may struggle with what to do and say, or how to act and feel. While there are **high stakes in how you handle these love challenges,** look at them also as opportunities to **strengthen** *your* **relationship with your child**.

Love Challenge Recap

Two overall tips for all love challenge discussions to keep in mind.

- Stay calm.

- Let your child know you are always there for them.

While we discussed strategies for different love challenges in this chapter, here's what to consider to preserve a good relationship with your child, while helping them with their love relationship(s):

- Set clear realistic expectations.

- Encourage special strengths of your child.

- Discuss present values and future goals.

- Respect differences between you and your child, and between you and your child's partner.

- Listen and ask questions.

- Don't judge or criticize your child's partner. Allow your child to discover any issues through your questions.

- Schedule special one-on-one time with your child.

Good Relationships for Your Children Start with You

Now is a very crucial point in your journey as a parent. The stakes are high and most importantly, *you have the power to change* your children's love relationships, and at the same time, pave the road to a better lifelong relationship with your children. *Good relationships for your children start with you.*

As you know from my story, I'm a Midwestern gal who grew up in a psychology-forward and relationship-oriented family. On a recent visit with my parents in Minneapolis, I asked them about their biggest concerns as parents when I was growing up. They talked about how they hoped that they were good role models of the kind of people and positive relationships they desired for me, my brother, and my sister. They wanted us to treat other people with appreciation and respect even if they were different than us. And honestly, I didn't prompt my mother at all, but she then mentioned how they also wanted us to be able to listen and *really hear* what others were saying and to understand that love partners could disagree and still care about one another. In other words, they consistently tried to emulate appreciation, respect, good communication, and handling conflict well with each other.

My father chimed in that they tried to have many conversations with us about those topics and the vital role that relationships play in life and happiness, even when we were young teenagers. He reminded me that as a family, we would often sit at the dinner table and my parents would ask: "What kinds of friends do you get along with the best?"; "What is it about your teacher/friend/partner that you really like?"; "Do you know what trust means?"; or "Do you think your mother and I agree on every topic?" At the time, I didn't enjoy these thought-provoking questions and I often wondered why I couldn't have parents who asked about television shows or sports teams, like my friends' parents seemed to do. But now, as I write this book and reflect about my childhood, I realize that my parents wanted these conversations to set the tone for my own personal relationships.

I really enjoyed hearing my parents' perspective during my recent visit. I recognized that these kinds of discussions with my parents—similar to the ones I have shared with you in this book to have with your children—bring me closer to my parents (even now!). And these types of conversations will do the same for you and your young adult child. Your children may not always show appreciation for these discussions, and I recognize that the conversations may not be easy to initiate, but they are the foundation for a long-term good relationship with your children.

A RECAP

We covered a lot in this book. Most importantly, the book combines three perspectives:

1. Good, science-based information from my own research and other high-quality studies.

2. Practical information, tips, quizzes, scripts, and easy-to-understand strategies to help you from my experiences as a therapist, coach, and workshop presenter.

3. Personal examples that I've tried or done as a parent and succeeded with.

You learned that in order for your young adult children to have happy, healthy love relationships it is crucial for you to **build trust** and help them set realistic relationship expectations because *frustration* is the leading reason that relationships are unhappy. You discovered how to begin what are likely to be the most important *conversations* you will have with your child, how to let go of your own *emotional baggage* about relationships, and ask the *right questions*. You also found out that *affirmation*, through words and actions, is a key factor in happy, healthy relationships. When your children receive that affirmation and give it to their love partners, they will be happier and their relationships will be more fulfilling.

Communication is vital to any happy, healthy love relationship. You now understand how different types of verbal and nonverbal communication affect the way we convey messages and receive them, and how you can model and have conversations with your child to fend off the types of *miscommunication* that can harm relationships. You learned about the role parents play in equipping their children with healthy coping behaviors to *handle stress and disagreements*, and a money vocabulary to talk and manage *financial issues*. You also discovered how to help your child meet and find love partners, make a big deal about *the right relationship*, and distinguish *lust from love*.

You now have effective tools to manage and survive specific love challenges with your young adult child, when you need them. If you haven't experienced these common challenges, the tips and strategies I provide will be there for you in the future. I've shared ways to address or deal with love challenges that will preserve your happy, healthy relationship with your child over the long haul *and* improve your child's love relationships.

FOUR KEY LESSONS

The big message for you is this: You picked up this book because you care about your children. You want them to be happy and experience healthy love relationships. You know the vital role that relationships play in your life and those of your children. The information you learned in this book *will* help you, as a parent, *survive* your children's love relationships and experience better, stronger relationships with your children. But whenever you get stuck or maybe a bit discouraged, return to the following **four key lessons from this book**:

1. **Practice** what is in the book and be a good role model.

2. **Use** the questions, discussions, exercises, quizzes, and simple strategies in this book to have deep conversations about love and relationships with your children.

3. **Provide** your children with probing questions to help them discover and recognize the important ingredients and challenges to happy, healthy love relationships.

4. **Understand** the science behind love and relationships.

As you know, I have two young adult children. My daughter is 27 years old and my son is 24 years old. Neither has yet found the right love partner. Both of them date and have experienced good love relationships. But they have also faced a few love relationships that weren't good or the best for them. Each time I've been proactive and talked to them about these relationships—both good and not so good, using the strategies and tools that I shared in this book. I've asked the questions. I've shared the science and the exercises. We've had the conversations. We've analyzed what happened. They have learned and grown from these experiences. But most importantly they haven't given up on love and relationships, and our parent-child bond has become stronger and closer (*and I think they would say that too*!).

DON'T WAIT!

The information in this book can't guarantee happy, healthy love relationships for your children. But you will see positive changes. The information will help you and your young adult children have better and stronger relationships, now and in the future. More trust. Less frustration. More conversations. More appreciation. Better communication. Better able to manage stress and conflict. More talk about money. More kindness. More connection. Better handling of challenges as they arise.

What are you waiting for? Use the simple practical strategies and tools in this book and start to apply them today! Implement what you learned and watch your children's love relationships bloom.

Endnotes

1   Paul R. Amato, "Research on Divorce: Continuing Trends and New Developments," *Journal of Marriage and Family* 72 no. 3 (2010): 650–666, http://dx.doi.org/10.1111/j.1741-3737.2010.00723.x; and Terri L. Orbuch, Joseph Veroff, Halimah Hassan, and Julie Horrocks, "Who Will Divorce: A 14-year Longitudinal Study of Black Couples and White Couples," *Journal of Social and Personal Relationships* 19 no. 2 (2002): 179–202, https://doi.org/10.1177/0265407502192002

2   Rowland S. Miller, *Intimate Relationships*, 9th ed. (New York: McGraw Hill, 2022). Compiled from several chapters in the textbook.

3   Guttmacher Institute, "Adolescent Sexual and Reproductive Health in the United States," fact sheet, September 2019, https://www.guttmacher.org/fact-sheet/american-teens-sexual-and-reproductive-health

4   Cindy M. Meston and David M. Buss, "Why Humans Have Sex," *Archives of Sexual Behavior*, 36 (2007): 477–507, https://doi.org/10.1007/s10508-007-9175-2

5   George Herbert Mead, *Mind, Self, and Society* (Chicago: University of Chicago Press, 1934).

6   Jeff Guo, "Researchers Have Found a Major Problem with 'The Little Mermaid' and Other Disney Movies," *The Washington Post*, January 25, 2016, https://www.washingtonpost.com/news/wonk/wp/2016/01/25/researchers-have-discovered-a-major-problem-with-the-little-mermaid-and-other-disney-movies/

7   Peggy C. Giordano, Wendi L. Johnson, Wendy D. Manning, and Monica A. Longmore, "Parenting in Adolescence and Young Adult Intimate Partner Violence," *Journal of Family Issues* 37, no. 4 (2016): 443–465, https://www.ncbi.nlm.nih.gov/pmc/articles/PMC4758994/; and Marni L. Kan, Susan M. McHale, and Ann C. Crouter, "Parental Involvement in Adolescent Romantic Relationships: Patterns and Correlates," *Journal of Youth and Adolescence* 37 (2008): 168–179, doi.org 10.1007/s10964-007-9185-3

8 Talia Cornelius, Jeffrey L. Birk, Donald Edmondson, and Joseph E. Schwartz, "Ambulatory Blood Pressure Response to Romantic Partner Interactions and Long-Term Cardiovascular Health Outcomes," *Psychosomatic Medicine* 82, no. 4 (2020): 393–401, https://dx.doi.org/10.1097%2FPSY.0000000000000793; Bert N. Uchino, John T. Cacioppo, and Janice K. Kiecolt-Glaser, "The Relationship between Social Support and Physiological Processes: A Review with Emphasis on Underlying Mechanisms and Implications for Health," *Psychological Bulletin* 119, no. 3 (1996): 488–531, https://pubmed.ncbi.nlm .nih.gov/8668748/https://pubmed.ncbi.nlm.nih.gov/8668748/; Timothy J. Loving, and David A. Sbarra, "Relationships and Health," in *APA Handbook of Personality and Social Psychology, Volume 3: Interpersonal Relations*, ed. Mario Mikulincer, Phillip R. Shaver, Jeffrey A. Simpson, and John F. Dovidio (Washington, DC: American Psychological Association, 2015), 151–176; and Sarah D. Pressman, Sheldon Cohen, Gregory E. Miller, Anita Barkin, Bruce S. Rabin, and John J. Treanor, "Loneliness, Social Network Size, and Immune Response to Influenza Vaccination in College Freshmen," *Health Psychology,* 24 no. 3 (2005): 297–306, https://doi.org/10.1037/0278-6133.24.3.297

9 Karen L. Fingerman, "Consequential Strangers and Peripheral Ties: The Importance of Unimportant Relationships," *Journal of Family Theory & Review* 1, no. 2 (2009): 69–86, https://doiorg.huaryu.kl.oakland.edu/10.1111 /j.1756-2589.2009.00010.x

10 Amanda J. Rose and Karen D. Rudolph, "A Review of Sex Differences in Peer Relationship Processes: Potential Trade-offs for the Emotional and Behavioral Development of Girls and Boys," *Psychological Bulletin* 132, no. 1 (2006): 98–131, http://dx.doi.org/10.1037/0033-2909.132.1.98; and Karin A. Martin, "Becoming a Gendered Body: Practices of Preschools." *American Sociological Review* 63, no. 4 (1998): 494–511, https://www.jstor.org/stable /2657264

11 Beverley Fehr, *Friendship Processes* (Thousand Oaks, CA: Sage, 1995).

12 Andrea Gardner, "The Power of Words," www.andreagardner.co.uk February 23, 2010, https://www.youtube.com/watch?v=Hzgzim5m7oU

13 Kim B. Serota and Timothy Levine, "A Few Prolific Liars: Variation in the Prevalence of Lying," *Journal of Language and Social Psychology* 34 (2015): 138–157.

14 Erin B. McClure, "A Meta-analytic Review of Sex Differences in Facial Expression Processing and Their Development in Infants, Children, and Adolescents," *Psychological Bulletin* 126, no. 3 (2000): 424–453, http://dx.doi.org/10.1037/0033-2909.126.3.424; Leslie R. Brody and Judith

A. Hall, "Gender, Emotion, and Socialization," in *Handbook of Gender Research in Psychology,* vol. 1, ed. Joan Chrisler and Donald R. McCreaty (New York: Springer, 2010), 429–454; and Judith A. Hall and Marianne Schmid Mast, "Are Women Always More Interpersonally Sensitive than Men? Impact of Goals and Content Domain," *Personality and Social Psychology Bulletin* 34, no. 1 (2008): 144–155, https://doi.org/10.1177/0146167207309192

15 Tanya Vacharkulksemsuk, Emily Reit, Poruz Khambatta, Paul W. Eastwick, Eli J. Finkel, and Dana R. Carney, "Dominant, Open Nonverbal Displays Are Attractive at Zero-acquaintance," *Proceedings of the National Academy of Sciences* 113, no. 15 (2016): 4009–4014, https://doi.org/10.1073/pnas.1508932113; and Yannick Stephan, Angelina R. Sutin, Gabriel Bovier-Lapierre, and Antonio Terracciano, "Personality and Walking Speed across Adulthood: Prospective Evidence from Five Samples," *Social Psychological and Personality Science* 9, no. 7 (2018): 773–780, https://doi.org/10.1177/1948550617725152

16 Daniel T. Cordaro, Rui Sun, Dacher Keltner, Shanmukh Kamble, Niranjan Huddar, and Galen McNeil, "Universals and Cultural Variations in 22 Emotional Expressions across Five Cultures," *Emotion* 18, no. 1 (2018): 75, https://doi.org/10.1037/emo0000302; and Hyisung C. Hwang and David Matsumoto, "Facial Expressions," in *APA Handbook of Nonverbal Communication*, ed. David Matsumoto, Hyisung C. Hwang, and Mark G. Frank (New York: American Psychological Association, 2016), 257–287.

17 Agnieszka Sorokowska, Piotr Sorokowski, Peter Hilpert, Katarzyna Cantarero, Tomasz Frackowiak, Khodabakhsh Ahmadi, ... and John D. Pierce Jr, "Preferred Interpersonal Distances: A Global Comparison," *Journal of Cross-Cultural Psychology* 48, no. 4 (2017): 577–592, https://doi.org/10.1177/0022022117698039

18 Amanda J. Rose and Karen D. Rudolph, "A Review of Sex Differences in Peer Relationship Processes: Potential Trade-offs for the Emotional and Behavioral Development of Girls and Boys," *Psychological Bulletin* 132, no. 1 (2006): 98–131, http://dx.doi.org/10.1037/0033-2909.132.1.98

19 Mayo Clinic, "Stress Relief from Laughter? It's No Joke," July 29, 2021, https://www.mayoclinic.org/healthy-lifestyle/stress-management/in-depth/stress-relief/art-20044456.

20 Paul R. Amato, "Reconciling Divergent Perspectives: Judith Wallerstein, Quantitative Family Research, and Children of Divorce," *Family Relations* 52, no. 4 (2003): 332–339, https://doi.org/10.1111/j.17413729.2003.00332.x

21 John M. Gottman, *What Predicts Divorce?* (Hillsdale, NJ: Erlbaum, 1994); and John M. Gottman and Robert W. Levenson, "The Timing of Divorce:

Predicting When a Couple Will Divorce over a 14-year Period," *Journal of Marriage and Family* 62, no. 3 (2000): 737–745, https://doi.org/10.1111 /j.1741-3737.2000.00737.x

22 Lauren M. Papp, "Topics of Marital Conflict in the Everyday Lives of Empty Nest Couples and Their Implications for Conflict Resolution," *Journal of Couple & Relationship Therapy* 17, no. 1 (2018): 7–24, https://doi.org/10.1080 /15332691.2017.1302377

23 Lynsey K. Romo, "Money Talks: Revealing and Concealing Financial Information in Families," *Journal of Family Communication* 11, no. 4 (2011): 264–281, https://doi.org/10.1080/15267431.2010.544634; and Liezel Alsemgeest, "Family Communication about Money: Why the Taboo?" *Mediterranean Journal of Social Sciences* 5, no. 16 (2014): 516, https://doi.org /10.5901/mjss.2014.v5n16p516

24 Melanie Hicken, "How to Talk about Money before Saying 'I do,'" CNN Money, June 13, 2013, https://money.cnn.com/2013/06/13/news/money -marriage/index.html

25 "Valpak® Survey Finds Savers, Not Spenders, Are the New Sexy," Cision PR Newswire, June 4, 2014, https://www.prnewswire.com/news-releases/valpak- survey-finds-savers-not-spenders-are-the-new-sexy-261875891.html

26 Consumer Financial Protection Bureau, "Money as You Grow," March 17, 2017, https://www.consumerfinance.gov/consumer-tools/money-as-you-grow/

27 Richard L. Moreland and Scott F. Beach, "Exposure Effects in the Classroom: The Development of Affinity among Students," *Journal of Experimental Social Psychology* 28 (1992): 255–276, https://doi.org/10.1016/0022-1031 (92)90055-O; and Kellan Mrkva and Leaf Van Boven, "Salience Theory of Mere Exposure: Relative Exposure Increases Liking, Extremity, and Emotional Intensity," *Journal of Personality and Social Psychology* 118, no. 6 (2020), http://dx.doi.org/10.1037/pspa0000184

28 Statista Research Department, "Number of Online Dating Users U.S. 2017– 2024," July 5, 2021, Statista, https://www.statista.com/statistics/417654 /us-online-dating-user-numbers/

29 Ellen Berscheid and Elaine Walster, "A Little Bit about Love," in *Foundations in Interpersonal Attraction*, ed. Theodore Huston (New York: Academic Press, 1974), 335–381; Bianca P. Acevedo and Arthur Aron, "Does a Long- term Relationship Kill Romantic Love?" *Review of General Psychology* 13, no. 1 (2009): 59–65, https://doi.org/10.1037/a0014226; Susan Sprecher and Pamela C. Regan, "Passionate and Companionate Love in Courting and Young Married Couples," *Sociological Inquiry* 68 (1998): 163–185, https://

onlinelibrary.wiley.com/doi/10.1111/j.1475-682X.1998.tb00459.x; and Donatella Marazziti, Hagop Akiskal, Alessandra Rossi, and G. B. Cassano, "Alteration of the Platelet Serotonin Transporter in Romantic Love," *Psychological Medicine* 29, no. 3 (1999): 741–745, https://doi.org/10.1017 /S0033291798007946

30 Ted L. Huston and Amy F. Chorost, "Behavioral Buffers on the Effect of Negativity on Marital Satisfaction: A Longitudinal Study," *Personal Relationships* 1 (1994): 223–239, https://doi.org/10.1111/j.1475-6811.1994 .tb00063.x; and Sylvia Niehuis, Alan Reifman, Du Feng, and Ted L. Huston, "Courtship Progression Rate and Declines in Expressed Affection Early in Marriage: A Test of the Disillusionment Model," *Journal of Family Issues* 37, no. 8 (2016): 1074–1100, https://doi.org/10.1177/0192513X14540159

31 Andrew Galperin and Martie Haselton, "Predictors of How Often and When People Fall in Love," *Evolutionary Psychology* 8, no. 1 (2010): 5–28, https://doi.org/10.1177/147470491000800102

32 Stanislav Treger and James N. Masciale, "Domains of Similarity and Attraction in Three Types of Relationships," *Interpersona* 12, no. 2 (2018): 254–266, http://dx.doi.org/10.5964/ijpr.v12i2.321; Robert Böhm, Astrid Schütz, Katrin Rentzsch, André Körner, and Friedrich Funke, "Are We Looking for Positivity or Similarity in a Partner's Outlook on Life? Similarity Predicts Perceptions of Social Attractiveness and Relationship Quality," *The Journal of Positive Psychology* 5, no. 6 (2010): 431–438, https://doi.org/10 .1080/17439760.2010.534105; and Marian M. Kito, M. I. E. Morry, and L. Ortiz, "The Attraction–Similarity Model and Dating Couples: Projection, Perceived Similarity, and Psychological Benefits," *Personal Relationships* 18 no. 1 (2011): 125–143, https://doi-org.huaryu.kl.oakland.edu/10.1111 /j.1475-6811.2010.01293.x

33 Mindy E. Scott, Nicole R. Steward-Streng, Jennifer Manlove, Erin Schelar, and Carol Cui, "Characteristics of Young Adult Sexual Relationships: Diverse, Sometimes Violent, Often Loving," *Child Trends* 18 (2011): 1–8, https://doi.org/10.1037/e506862011-001

34 Brian J. Willoughby, Jason S. Carroll, and Dean M. Busby, "Differing Relationship Outcomes when Sex Happens before, on, or after First Dates," *Journal of Sex Research* 51 (2014): 52–61, https://doi-org.huaryu.kl.oakland .edu/10.1080/00224499.2012.714012; Deborah Davis, Phillip R. Shaver, Keith F. Widaman, Michael L. Vernon, William C. Follette, and Kendra Beitz, "I Can't Get No Satisfaction: Insecure Attachment, Inhibited Sexual Communication, and Sexual Dissatisfaction," *Personal Relationships* 13, no. 4 (2006): 465–483, https://doi-org.huaryu.kl.oakland.

edu/10.1111/j.1475-6811.2006.00130.x; David A. Frederick, Janet Lever, Brian Joseph Gillespie, and Justin R. Garcia, "What Keeps Passion Alive? Sexual Satisfaction Is Associated with Sexual Communication, Mood Setting, Sexual Variety, Oral Sex, Orgasm, and Sex Frequency in a National US Study," *The Journal of Sex Research* 54, no. 2 (2017): 186–201, https://doi.org/10.1080/00224499
.2015.1137854; and E. Sandra Byers and Sheila MacNeil, "The Relationships between Sexual Problems, Communication, and Sexual Satisfaction," *The Canadian Journal of Human Sexuality* 6, no. 4 (1997): 277, https://www.proquest.com/scholarly-journals/relationships-between-sexual-problems/docview/220816794/se-2?accountid=12924

35 Monica Anderson, Emily A. Vogels, and Erica Turner, *The Virtues and Downsides of Online Dating* (Washington, DC: Pew Research Center, February 6, 2020), https://www.pewresearch.org/internet/2020/02/06/the-virtues-and-downsides-of-online-dating/

About the Author

Dr. Terri Orbuch (PhD) is a Distinguished Professor at Oakland University, research scientist at University of Michigan's Institute for Social Research, and an author, speaker, date and relationship coach, therapist, and The Love Doctor® in the media. Her practical, science-based advice has helped thousands of people find and create the loving relationships they deserve. She is the director of a landmark study, funded by the National Institutes of Health (NIH), where she has been following the same couples for more than three decades.

Dr. Orbuch has been featured in such national publications as *The New York Times*, *Wall Street Journal*, *Reader's Digest*, *USA Today*, *Women's Health*, *Cosmopolitan*, and *TIME* magazine and has appeared on *The Today Show*, MSNBC, *The Katie Couric Show*, ESPN, *HuffPost Live*, and CNN. Her national public television special is called "Secrets from The Love Doctor" and her TEDx talk, "Is It Lust or Is It Love?" has more than 2.8 million views. She brings simple, straightforward, science-based relationship advice to real people everywhere. She lives in Michigan with her husband. For more information, please go to: DrTerriTheLoveDoctor.com.

www.ingramcontent.com/pod-product-compliance
Lightning Source LLC
Chambersburg PA
CBHW062157080426
42734CB00010B/1721